Communion Meditations

Outlines and Messages

George Gritter

PULPIT LIBRARY

BAKER BOOK HOUSE
Grand Rapids, Michigan 49506

Contents

Preface

How many and great are the blessings we enjoy! As we thank God for them, we realize that we are not as grateful as we ought to be.

Could this be particularly true with regard to the Lord's Supper? Holy Communion with God and his people, is there anything more blessed on earth?

Do we at times fail to experience that blessedness because our observance of the Lord's Supper has become routine, or because we are vexed by a deep-seated uneasiness? Sometimes misgivings rather than assurance fill our soul.

Holy Communion often fails to bring the comfort and joy that we seek. We know that the fault lies in ourselves, not in others, and surely not in God.

These meditations are presented in the hope that they will assist pastors, congregations, and individuals, in a holy exercise of faith which will be to their benefit and to God's praise.

1

Rest for the Weary

Come to me, all you who are weary and burdened, and I will give you rest. Take my yoke upon you and learn from me, for I am gentle and humble in heart, and you will find rest for your souls. For my yoke is easy, and my burden is light (Matt. 11:28 – 30).

A. Gracious Invitation
   1. Echoing previous revelation
   2. Expressing divine concern
B. Obvious Need
   1. Apparent in the world
   2. Understood by Jesus
C. Beautiful Promise
   1. Divine
   2. Blessed
D. Enlightening Admonition
   1. Learn of me
   2. Take my yoke upon you

Gracious Invitation

"Come unto me." What a beautiful invitation for people living in a suffering, burdened world! A world marked by indifference and rejection where outstretched hands find little response and pleading cries go unanswered.

The words are simple, the meaning is unmistakable. Anyone who struggles with problems or difficulties and seeks relief, is urged to come to Jesus.

This invitation echoes the call of God so repeatedly expressed in previous revelation. The Bible overflows with words of grace that are summarized in this benevolent text: "Cast your cares on the Lord and he will sustain you, . . ." (Ps. 55:22). Here something is added. We are not only promised strength to endure, but also the blessing of relief.

God does not remain at a distance. He who is high above us as Lord of all is also with us as our loving Father and gracious Savior. He came to us in his Son Jesus Christ to reveal himself as the God of deliverance. He does not intend that our struggles continue indefinitely, surely not eternally. Burdens will be lifted and ordeals will be terminated. Gathered round his word and seated at his table we hear his voice, feel his presence, and experience his grace. How wonderful to commune with God and how amazing that such communion is even possible! Jesus opened the way. He continues to say: Come unto me!

Obvious Need

To Jesus, the great need of men and the world was apparent. This eleventh chapter of Matthew underscores John the Baptist's doubt concerning Jesus' messiahship, the fickle and critical attitude of the multitude toward his message, and the persistent impenitence of those cities where Jesus had performed most of his mighty works. Confronted with these reactions to his ministry, would Jesus have been justified in bidding farewell, leaving men to the consequences of their own attitudes and actions? When men doubt the message, why continue to proclaim it? When men refuse salvation, why continue to offer it?

But Jesus came on a mission of mercy; he remained sensitive to the needs of those who are lost and persisted in his efforts to save. This was his Father's will. So, as he did before, he raised his voice in a pleading invitation, "Come unto me." He understands men better than they understand themselves.

Picture for a moment the world in which Jesus lived — the donkey with a heavy load on its back, the camel transporting an even greater cargo, and people weighted with yokes on their shoulders or carrying vessels and baskets on their heads. What a life of stress and strain!

And everywhere Jesus saw the deaf, the blind, the lame, the leprous, the poor, and the oppressed. But the greatest burdens of all were those weighing on hearts and minds: questions people could not answer, problems they could not solve, conditions they could not change, and hearts they could not heal. The Lord of life had come into a dying world.

Never could Jesus remain indifferent because the heart of God is not calloused. He was moved with infinite compassion and as the great physician he healed all manner of diseases. He performed deeds of might and mercy, and miracles of grace; he provided blessed relief and signified that He came to deal with the underlying cause — to lift the burden of sin. He was God's answer to a universal need; He is the sinner's only hope of salvation.

Beautiful Promise

The throbbing invitation is accompanied with the thrilling promise, "I will give you rest." All who turn to Christ, realizing and confessing their need, will find in him what they can find nowhere else. Only the Son of God can give peace and satisfaction. Rescue from sin is beyond human power; all our efforts are bound to fail. As Saint Augustine exclaimed long ago, "Our hearts are restless until they rest in Thee."

Happily the serenity Jesus graciously provides need not be earned. It is not based on merit but is a gift of grace. Notice, Jesus says, "I will *give* you rest."

But why then are we still troubled and ill at ease? We know the answer. We know it from God's word and from our own conscience. Though saved we are still imperfect. We are inconsistent, faulty in our obedience, and weak in faith. How we wish we could be more pleasing to God! What shall we do? We look to God for grace, strength, and encouragement. We find our consolation and hope in the cross; and with the vision of it clearly before our eyes here at the Lord's Table, we believe that we are forgiven.

Enlightening Admonition

The gracious invitation and promise of Jesus are accompanied by an enlightening injunction, "Take my yoke upon you, and learn from me . . . and you will find rest for your souls. . . ." Contradictory as it may seem, the "rest" we already possess must yet be found.

What does that mean? Perhaps an illustration will help us understand. Parents are blessed with a child and are thankful for the priceless privilege of caring for him or her. That child is a gift of God; the child is theirs. But it is only as days and years go by that the abundance of God's favor becomes more apparent. So it is with the rest which Jesus gives. It grows, and day by day we grow in appreciation and experience of its blessedness.

You say that you wish that were true in your case? You are not alone in feeling that way. That is why Jesus gives enlightening instruction; He points the way to greater tranquility.

To take his yoke means to submit to his guidance and authority, to let him choose the way and to follow him in it. We receive rest by faith and enter more fully into it by obedience. We grow in assurance and comfort when we recognize and honor our Savior as the Lord of our lives.

That seems difficult — and it is. But when we learn how gentle and humble our Savior is, appreciating the greatness of his love, experiencing his gentle care, and being influenced by his perfect example, his yoke becomes easy. Duty becomes desire. Willing "followship" becomes joyful fellowship.

To the extent that we fail to live the Christian life we are disappointed with ourselves. And we should be. But though at times we are discouraged we need never despair. God who gave us faith will also strengthen it. You may be confident "that he who began a good work in you will carry it on to completion until the day of Jesus Christ" (Phil. 1:6). All who come to God for salvation and continue to come for the grace they need shall never be turned away. That grace is offered in both Word and Sacrament.

At the Lord's table we join with fellow-believers in the beautifully responsive verse:

> I heard the voice of Jesus say,
> "Come unto me and rest;
> Lay down, thou weary one, lay down
> Thy head upon my breast."
>
> I came to Jesus as I was,
> Weary, and worn, and sad,
> I found in Him a resting place,
> And he has made me glad.
>
> Horatius Bonar, 1846

And we know that the rest which we have in Christ is ours forever. Our sins are forgiven, our burdens will be lifted, and our struggles must end. Think, delight yourself in the simple but very precious promise, "There remains then a Sabbath rest for the people of God . . ." (Heb. 4:9).

2

Jesus, Savior of Sinners

Here is a trustworthy saying that deserves full acceptance: Christ Jesus came into the world to save sinners—of whom I am the worst (1 Tim. 1:15).

A. Gloriously True
1. The message of the gospel
2. The challenge to all who hear
3. The experience of Paul
4. The conviction of believers
B. Simply Stated
1. Jesus Christ *came*
2. He *came into the world*
3. He *came to save*
C. Humbly Confessed
1. Humility required by God
2. Humility necessitated by our unworthiness
3. Humility demonstrated by deep contrition
4. Humility intensified by fellowship with God

On this, the Lord's Day, we as God's people are gathered in God's house, around God's word. Today an added privilege is ours—we may sit at the Lord's table with fellow-believers and with Christ himself. How wonderful to be children of God, members of his family! May we experience a full measure of divine blessing as we dwell on the message which the gospel proclaims and the Lord's Supper portrays: Jesus, Savior of sinners.

Gloriously True

Yes, we have a wonderful gospel but only those who believe it experience its saving power. Many who have heard the word have remained indifferent or hostile. And the sterner side of God's truth is that those who fail to respond in faith remain under divine judgment. To sinners comes the call: Repent and believe. That is the call sincerely and earnestly presented to you now if you do not know Jesus as your personal Savior. The Bible says we are lost and we must confess it.

The gospel challenges us to believe the unbelievable. Sometimes we are troubled by doubts and fears because the message seems too good to be true.

Paul himself had resisted. To him the thought that Jesus was the promised messiah, the Savior of the world, was ridiculous, even blasphemous. Paul hated the gospel and persecuted the church, but by God's grace he was brought to the light. Confronted by the risen and living Lord, Paul was convinced of Jesus' true identity and mission.

The Bible leaves no doubt about the Messiah. Before Mary's Son was born she and Joseph were told that his name would be Jesus, meaning Savior. The angelic messenger specifically underscores the reason for that name by declaring ". . . he will save his people from their sins" (Matt. 1:21b). And that is also the message to the shepherds in Ephrata's fields, "Today in the town of David a Savior has been born to you; he is Christ the Lord" (Luke 2:11).

Paul, too, is a chosen and chief emissary of the gospel. As such he has witnessed a marvellous demonstration of its saving power. Thousands of people have believed and hundreds of churches have been established.

Now we understand why Paul refers to a "trustworthy saying." The power and truth of the gospel have gained wide recognition. The conviction that God's word is reliable and His grace is sure is becoming increasingly accepted and more widespread.

Will you come to the Lord's Table with that assurance? Perhaps the eagerness in your soul is tempered or restrained. You wish you had greater certainty. The fact is that the Lord understands that feeling. He knows better than you do that your faith is not yet what it ought to be. And it is for that very reason that he has given you the Lord's Supper and invites you to partake—that your faith may be strengthened and your assurance may grow.

Simply Stated

Paul, inspired by the Holy Spirit, expresses the gospel with beautiful clarity: Christ Jesus came into the world to save sinners. Think of it! The Son of God left the glories of heaven. He desired to do this because it was the Father's will. That is the message summarized for us in those best-known and most-loved words of Scripture, "For God so loved the world that he gave his one and only Son, that whoever believes in him shall not perish but have eternal life" (John 3:16).

Christ Jesus came into the world, a world so sinful that anyone except the Son would have hesitated. And well they might; for there was not a thing mortals could do to change conditions or alleviate the misery. Only God could do that.

And God is not indifferent. He is the God of love and the world is his creation. He did not intend that it should self-destruct. He sees the misery on earth. He sees that mothers sigh, babies cry, and sinners die. And in the greatness of his love moved with infinite compassion, he sent his Son as the answer to the world's need. He is the God of judgment, but also the God of salvation.

And so when Jesus came, he came to save. He did not come to pay a visit, then return to heaven with the report that all was hopeless. No, as John in his Gospel declares: "He lived among us"—he saw, he heard, he cared and shared. As the "Man of Sorrows" he identified with us in all things, except sin.

Yes, Jesus has been here; he knows our condition, our trials and disappointments, our hurts, our pains, our frustrations. He knows our sin and reminds us in his word and sacrament that he came to take it away. He was sent by the Father with a specific purpose and nothing could deter him from fulfilling that mission—to rescue us from misery and condemnation.

And consider the cost! Born in a stable, residing in a nondescript town under primitive conditions inconceivable to us, enduring unspeakable reproach and shame, he finally died on Calvary's cross where his blood was shed as the price of our redemption.

Today this is brought clearly to mind; we look to the cross to experience anew its comfort and power, and to drink deeply from the fountain of eternal life.

Humbly Confessed

"God opposes the proud but gives grace to the humble" (James 4:6b). God gives grace to sinners who confess their sins and to saints who confess their unworthiness. The more intimate our fellowship with God, the more we realize that we are undeserving. We begin to understand why Paul, that great saint, considered himself the chief of sinners. And when we compare ourselves with the demands of both the law and the gospel, there are times when we feel exactly the same way.

The joy of salvation and the sorrow for sin are not contradictory. They go hand in hand. We have peace not because we are good, but because we are forgiven.

So as believers we draw near to God with a deep sense of contrition. We pour out our souls in penitent confession, we admit our personal need, and we present our pleading prayers. Both Word and sacrament assure us that our confession is heard, our need fulfilled, and our prayer answered—all for the sake of Jesus Christ our Savior.

On the gravestone of a missionary who devoted his life to telling others the story of the gospel is inscribed this epitaph: "The Savior bids you come to Him." Is not that the constant call of the gospel? And having come to him for salvation, we come to him again and again for continued blessing.

You are present here today by divine invitation. Do not permit anything to interfere with the blessing which is yours, having been merited for you by Christ. As you humbly confess your sin, humbly confess your faith, and magnify Jesus Christ your Savior:

> Thou, O Christ, art all I want;
>   More than all in thee I find.
> Raise the fallen, cheer the faint,
>   Heal the sick, and lead the blind.
> Just and holy is thy Name
>   I am all unrighteousness;
> False and full of sin I am,
>   Thou art full of truth and grace.
>
> Plenteous grace with thee is found,
>   Grace to cover all my sin;
> Let the healing streams abound,
>   Make me, keep me pure within—
> Thou of life the fountain art,
>   Freely let me take of thee;
> Spring thou up within my heart,
>   Rise to all eternity.
>   Charles Wesley, 1740

3

The Blood of the Covenant

*This is my blood of the covenant, which is poured out
for many for the forgiveness of sins* (Matt. 26:28).

A. **"This Is My Blood"**
  1. The significance
  2. Jesus' anticipation
B. **"This Is My Blood of the Covenant"**
  1. God's covenant with Adam
  2. Fulfillment in the cross
C. **"My Blood . . . Poured Out for Many"**
  1. An expression of love
  2. Numbered among the saved
D. **". . . For the Forgiveness of Sins"**
  1. A price too steep
  2. The price is paid
  3. Remembrance of the sacrifice

The Words of Jesus

Listen to the words of Jesus as he gathered with his disciples in the Upper Room. To the Twelve, they were an indication of what was about to happen; to us they are an interpretation of what actually did happen.

Before instituting the sacred supper Jesus celebrated the Passover, a memorial of the deliverance of God's people from the bondage of Egypt and, at the same time, symbolic and prophetic of a greater deliverance to come. Men are not really free until they are free from sin.

Through long and oppressive centuries, hope had been kept alive. God's children suffer because they live in a sinful world, and because they themselves transgress, but the day of salvation is sure. What God has promised he will do. When the Messiah comes, burdens will be lifted and men shall be set free from the bondage of sin. Now that day has come; the hour is here.

Jesus took the cup, gave thanks, and offered it to his disciples using words, the meaning of which they did not fully comprehend. What did he say and what do his words signify? He proclaimed the very heart of the gospel. Listen and pray that God will bring us understanding.

"This Is My Blood"

The cup and the wine have profound significance. They speak of God's love as revealed in the gift of his Son. For centuries sacrifices and offerings were brought to underscore the unalterable truth that guilty sinners deserve the penalty of death. They can be rescued only by one who offers a sacrifice of infinite worth on their behalf and dies in their stead. But who can accomplish such a task? Who can bring such a sacrifice? Not you, or I, or anyone else.

> Not all the blood of beasts
>   On Jewish altars slain
> Could give the guilty conscience peace
>   Or wash away the stain.
> But Christ, the heavenly Lamb,
>   Takes all our guilt away;
> A sacrifice of nobler name
>   And richer blood than they.
>   Isaac Watts, 1709

The time has come for that blood to be shed. It is the Great Day of Atonement, the day the Son of God will offer himself as the sacrifice for the sins of men. He will pay the price, break the shackles, and set men free. The wine poured into the cup represents his shed blood, his supreme and perfect sacrifice on the cross.

Jesus was not surprised by Calvary. He was aware that he had come into the world to die, to offer himself in our stead; he knew himself to be the chosen Lamb of God.

He alone, knew what that meant. That very night his soul would be overwhelmed with sorrow, his sweat falling as drops of blood to the ground. And in anguish he would pray, "Father, if it is possible, may this cup be taken from me. Yet not as I will, but as you will" (Matt. 26:39).

Yes, Jesus realized that a terrible ordeal awaited Him. He would be arrested, tried, condemned, and crucified. That ordeal was very near, only a few hours away, but undaunted he said to his disciples, "This my blood." Willingly, voluntarily, completely he will offer his life for theirs. The good shepherd lays down his life for his sheep.

This Is my Blood of the Covenant"

The covenant to which Jesus referred is the relationship of love which existed between God and man in Paradise. God created Adam in his own image and for holy fellowship and service. Luke 3:37 refers to Adam as "the son of God." Tragically that covenant was broken when Adam and Eve yielded to temptation and transgressed the commandment of God.

But God did not forsake his fallen creature, his erring child. He caught him up in his arms with infinite compassion and promised that the original relationship would be restored by a redeemer described as "the seed of the woman." That promise first made to Adam, repeated to the patriarchs, confirmed and enriched by the message of the prophets, is now fulfilled in Christ.

The central theme of the gospel is salvation through Jesus

Christ because through the cross the power of sin and Satan is broken and grace is proclaimed to sinners. The blood of Christ is the blood of reconciliation which restores us and makes us "right with God." Then we shall never be lost but shall be blest forever.

This Jesus foresaw. His death would bring salvation. Of that he was sure and in that prospect he rejoiced; we begin to understand that he looked to the cross with sadness but also looked beyond it with gladness as indicated by the words, ". . . who for the joy set before him endured the cross, scorning its shame . . ." (Heb. 12:2).

"My Blood . . . Poured Out for Many"

Jesus had said, "I am the good shepherd," and had added, "The good shepherd lays down his life for his sheep." That will happen when his skin is lacerated with cruel scourging, when blood flows from his thorn-crowned brow and from his nail-pierced hands and feet.

But his death certainly did not occur because he was a helpless victim in the hands of his enemies. He is the Son of God who chose to die to fulfil his Father's purpose to save sinners from their tragic condition and its horrible consequence. As he poured wine into the cup so he will pour out his blood. That is the supreme expression of his love for a holy God and unholy sinners.

Men are saved by divine mercy, not by human effort. God has planned and opens the way through Jesus who knows that his sacrifice will not be in vain. The seemingly barren tree of the cross will bear abundant and wonderful fruit. A lost world is reconciled to God; sinners are saved!

Christ's blood is poured out for many. The Father already knows them and the last judgment will reveal who they are. How many will come? No one knows. The Bible declares there will be a great multitude which no man can count, all of whom are washed and made clean in the blood of the Lamb.

You remember that once the disciples inquired about the number of those who would be saved. Instead of answering that question Jesus challenged them to ask themselves whether or not their own names were written in the book of life. Was their faith real? Were they assured of their own salvation? Did they truly acknowledge God's grace?

So it must be with us. We rejoice in the fact that the number of the saved will be greater than we now know or can imagine, but we ask ourselves if we are one of that number.

". . . for the Forgiveness of Sins"

Our transgressions against God and men are more than we can count and beyond our powers of reckoning—here is the problem we cannot solve, the question to which we have no answer.

But that which is impossible for men, is possible with God. God is never frustrated. A sinful world is under his control and evil men are not beyond his powers of reclamation. To be sure, a price must be paid but when no one else is able or willing to pay that price God comes to the rescue. He sent his Son to pay the ransom so that all who believe in him may be redeemed from their hopeless and lost condition.

Forgiveness! This is the gospel Jesus proclaimed. Multitudes heard the message, needy and penitent sinners were offered that assurance. Indeed that gospel is good news. It does not demand that we earn salvation or merit divine pardon. It emphasizes that grace is full and free.

But do not misunderstand. Grace is free but it is not cheap. It cost Jesus his life; He paid the incomprehensible price. He knew what was required and he persevered along the *via dolorosa* (the way of suffering), until all barriers were removed that we might come to God who first came to us. Jesus opened the way for us to follow and, as he himself declared, he was and is the Way.

What a wonderful story! What wondrous love! I remember how a beloved colleague expressed this amazing grace and I hope that with me you too will treasure his words:

> Wondrous Salvation!
>   The Father *thought it*
>   The Son *bought it*
>   The Holy Spirit *wrought it*
>   and by grace
>   I *sought it.*

Remember what Jesus the risen Lord so triumphantly declared to two puzzled disciples on the way to Emmaus on that first Easter Sunday. He predicted, "Repentance and forgiveness of sins will be preached in his name to all nations, beginning at Jerusalem" (Luke 24:47).

Have you heard that message and have you experienced its saving power? What joy it can bring to your soul and you long to hear his words again and again! How blessed you and I are that at the table of the Lord we may partake of bread and wine, the symbols of his sacrifice and hear our Savior say: "My son, my daughter, your sins are forgiven. Go and sin no more."

> Marvelous grace of our loving Lord,
> Grace that exceeds our sin and our guilt,
> Yonder on Calvary's mount out-poured,
> There where the blood of the lamb was spilt.
>
> Grace, grace, God's grace.
> Grace that will pardon and cleanse within;
> Grace, grace, God's grace,
> Grace that is greater than all our sin.
>   Julia H. Johnston, 1910

4

Of Sin and Grace

> Then Nathan said to David, "You are the man!"
> (2 Sam. 12:7a).
>
> Then David said to Nathan, "I have sinned against
> the Lord!" Nathan replied, "The Lord has taken away
> your sin. You are not going to die" (2 Sam. 12:13).

A. Sin Uncovered
  1. David has sinned
  2. David refuses to confess
  3. God will not let him go
B. Sin Confessed
  1. Prompted by God's message
  2. With growing conviction
  3. In pleading prayer
  4. A personal reminder
C. Sin Forgiven
  1. God's message
  2. Believer's assurance

W hat is it that we desire more than anything else in life? That question elicits a wide variety of answers, but ultimately there is one basic longing in the hearts of us all—we want to be happy. Hence we reach out and strive for those things which appear to make that possible.

Are you a happy person? That all depends—for true and abiding happiness cannot be found unless one is right with

God. But can we be right with God when all of us must admit that we are imperfect? The fact is that such acceptance from God is not only possible, but is a blessed reality.

Penitence is the road to pardon and peace. When we confess our sins and are assured that they are forgiven, we find more than happiness. We experience blessedness in God's favor and fellowship.

Admittedly it is not easy for us to confess our own sin and guilt. Personal bias and a sense of pride prompt us to ignore our faults or to engage in self-justification. It is easy to find excuses. We fail to see ourselves as we really are and we hesitate to travel the avenue of contrition which is both unpleasant and difficult. But travel it we must, not just once, but again and again. Confession of sin and experience of grace go hand in hand. Scripture illustrates this truth in the life of David. What a spiritual giant he was and how much we owe him for the example he set and for the lessons he taught us in the inspired psalms which flowed from his pen! David enriched us with messages for all situations and for every occasion.

Sin Uncovered

David was a true believer but the Bible does not hide the fact that he committed grievous sins. He was indeed "the man after God's own heart," but at times he walked in his own willful way. How discouraged you and I would be if Scripture remained silent concerning the sins of the saints! We would conclude that they merited God's favor but that for us who so often fall into sin there is no hope.

So we are told very candidly that David wandered from the path of righteousness and fell into deep transgression. Evil desire led to evil deeds. Guilty of gross immorality with Bathsheba, he connived to bring about the death of her husband Uriah in a vain attempt to hide his crime. As a result he was also guilty of murder.

We are shocked by this sordid chapter in David's life and we sense the warning articulated in the New Testament and intended for all, "So, if you think you are standing firm, be careful that you don't fall" (1 Cor. 10:12). Not one of us is a match for the devil. How earnestly we should pray, "Lord, lead us not into temptation."

Tragically, David compounded his guilt. Troubled by what he had done, he nevertheless refused to confess his evil deeds. He was concerned about his high standing and reputation. He felt he could not afford to make a clean breast of his terrible entanglement.

And so his lips remained silent as he refused to listen to the voice within him. And all the while there was a restlessness in his soul which robbed him of peace with God and with himself. He tried to convince himself that in time men would forget and that God would overlook his reprehensible conduct.

He knew better, of course, but for weeks and months he continued his stubborn resistance. To others it was evident that he was miserable but either they dared not admonish him, or he would not listen. If left to himself David would grow calloused, bitter, and even defiant. That could not happen. God in heaven sees his erring servant, takes pity on him, and will not let him go.

God sent Nathan the prophet who related a striking parable which prompted David to react in wrath and judgment toward the one who had dealt nefariously with his neighbor. It is then that David's blind spot was removed and he saw himself as God saw him. How pointed the accusation: "You are the man." David was exposed; his sin was uncovered.

Those who could know peace can never find it through denial of their sins and shortcomings. All men are sinners, and you and I are no exception. We must hear His holy commandments; we must look into the mirror of God's perfect law and see ourselves as we really are. Then we will turn to God with a humble recognition of our great need. This is the first step to reconciliation and to the assurance that God is our Father, and we are truly his children.

Sin Confessed

The manner in which David was brought to conviction of sin and confession of guilt was so direct that it seems almost brutal. After David himself judged that the man described in Nathan's parable was deserving of death the prophet declared: "You are the man." God was very patient with David but finally resorted to spiritual surgery which was bound to hurt. He did so not to be cruel but because it was necessary.

And it had an immediate effect. David advanced no argument or excuse. He made no attempt to place the blame on someone else. He simply said, "I have sinned." There it was — a sincere and humble confession. The king of Israel had been brought to his knees, he had no place to hide or to turn, he could only cast himself on the mercy of God.

And this he did. Once he admitted to himself and God how terribly he had sinned, he poured out his soul in a torrent of sorrow and pleaded for mercy. Listen to the psalm to which this experience gave birth. Likely you are well-acquainted with the tear-stained words:

> Have mercy on me, O God, . . .
> Wash away my iniquity
>   and cleanse me from all my sin!
> For I know my transgressions,
>   and my sin is always before me.
> Create within me a pure heart, O God,
>   and renew a steadfast spirit within me.
> Do not cast me from your presence
>   or take your Holy spirit from me.
> Restore to me the joy of your salvation, . . .
>   Psalm 51: 1a, 2 – 3, 10 – 12a

Such outpouring of thought and feeling is very painful, but also very blessed. It relieves the pressure; it has a cleansing effect. It leads to restoration and comfort, for the Lord hears the cry of the distressed and he restores the brokenhearted.

Do you see something, even much, of yourself in this portrayal of David? Is it not true that at times we are insensitive to the extent of our sin? We pride ourselves on being decent, law-abiding citizens; we are reliable and honest, we try to be considerate. Then what is wrong?

Just this, Jesus says that in the final day of judgment many shall consider themselves qualified for heaven and candidates for eternal glory. That assumption is based on their own merits. They were unquestionably decent and very religious but had never felt the need of Christ as their Savior from sin.

We must be awakened to our condition of need. Sinners in the sight of God need salvation and can be saved only by grace. That is why the prophets of old thundered against all apostasy and pleaded with Israel to return. That is why John the Baptist, herald of Messiah's coming, warned of impending judgment and called for repentance and faith. That is why Jesus castigated individuals and cities for their impenitence. That is why, in the same breath with its gracious appeal, the gospel also threatens condemnation: "Whoever believes and is baptized will be saved, but whoever does not believe will be condemned" (Mark 16:16).

Do you know yourself as a sinner? Do you know Jesus as your Savior? Then draw near to God with a humble, penitent spirit, eager to receive his blessing and to hear once again that your sins are forgiven. You are welcome; you will not be turned away. God will fulfill all your needs.

Sin Forgiven

Nathan had been given a demanding and difficult task. I wonder if he hesitated to perform it. I am convinced that he proceeded with a heavy heart, maybe even with a measure of fear. How would the king of Israel react to the stern rebuke he must bring? Yet he had no choice but to obey God. A prophet of the Lord must bring the message God had given him to speak.

But when that message was met with humble acceptance and when he heard the abject confession, "I have sinned," the prophet took heart. He was happy for Nathan knew that God the Lord had opened David's eyes and heart to his true condition. Men cannot change their skin and the leopard cannot change his spots, but the Lord can change the hearts of men. It is by the grace of God that men are brought to awareness of sin and then to assurance of salvation.

What was the divine response to David's simple and sincere confession? It was immediate and blessedly reassuring. Here it is: Nathan replied, "The Lord has taken away your sin." Though serious consequences would remain, judgment was removed. David could rest assured that he was right with God. He was saved, saved from his terrible shame and crushing distress; he was restored to God's favor and fellowship. As before, they would walk together.

God is a forgiving God, the God of all grace. He does not disregard those who call on him; He never turns a deaf ear to the penitent's humble plea for pardon. Of this David was assured, and in this he learned to rejoice. For if this experience gave birth to the broken-hearted confession of Psalm 51, it also bore fruit in the exultant words of the first two verses of Psalm 32:

> Blessed is he
> whose trangressions are forgiven,
> whose sins are covered.
> Blessed is the man
> whose sin the Lord does not count against him
> and in whose spirit is no deceit.

The message of God's word is the message of sin and grace. Those who deny their sins and continue in them shall surely perish. But those who acknowledge their transgressions shall surely be forgiven.

The gospel proclaims and the sacraments confirm that with God there is salvation and eternal life. Those for whom Christ died shall never die; they are forgiven once and for all. They are blessed in life and in death, because for them the end of life is a new beginning. The sting of death has been removed so that for God's children death is the gateway to glory.

Mourn then for the transgressions you commit, but rejoice in the Lord! Sing, yes sing, unto the Lord, the God of our salvation:

> My sin — O the bliss of this glorious thought! —
> My sin, not in part, but the whole,
> Is nailed to the cross and I bear it no more;
> Praise the Lord, praise the Lord, O my soul!
>   Horatio G. Spafford

5

Athirst for God

"As the deer pants for streams of water
  so my soul pants for you, O God.
My soul thirsts for God, for the living God (Ps. 42:1,
2a)
  On the last and greatest day of the Feast, Jesus stood
and said in a loud voice, "If a man is thirsty, let him
come to me and drink" (John 7:37).

A. The Soul's Deep Longing
   1. Expressed by the psalmist
   2. Intensified by trial
   3. Symbolized by the hunted deer
   4. Present in the believer's heart
B. God's Loving Concern
   1. As demonstrated in the wilderness
   2. As proclaimed by Jesus
      a) During the Feast of Tabernacles
      b) By a stirring invitation
C. The Emphatic Declaration
   1. As stated to the Samaritan woman
   2. A challenge to the exercise of faith
   3. Its twofold meaning
      a) We are refreshed
      b) We become a source of refreshment to others
D. The Required Response
   1. Heeding the invitation
   2. Testifying of experienced grace
   3. Rest in the divine assurance

The Soul's Deep Longing

The psalmist has a deep longing, an unquenchable desire in his soul. He needs God; his whole being cries out for renewal and fellowship which means strength, joy, and peace.

We do not know who wrote this psalm. The Bible does not always satisfy our curiosity; it *does* satisfy our need by telling us what we must know. If we do not know the psalmist's name, we at least know his situation as reflected in the thoughts he shares and the feelings he lays bare.

Evidently he is an exile in a strange land. Missing familiar surroundings which had been so precious to him, he longs for home. But most of all he longs for the house of God where he had experienced sweet communion with his maker and king. When this is indicated by the expression on his face, his enemies mock him; and when he turns to God in prayer, it seems as if there is no answer. He feels lonely and helpless.

All the while the psalmist's longing increases in intensity. He compares himself to a deer wearied and frightened by the pursuit of hunters; thirsting, panting for waters of a refreshing stream, without which he will surely die. So this believer needs God, needs him very much; he longs for the living God, the one who, in contrast to the idols and deities with which the psalmist is surrounded in a foreign land, is the author and sustainer of life, able to quench the believer's thirst.

What do you have in common with this unnamed child of God? One similarity is obvious, for God's word tells us that we are pilgrims and strangers on earth or, as Peter states it in the opening words of his First Epistle, we are "God's elect, strangers in the world. . . ."

But do we also share the psalmist's longing? Do we know the intense desire for fellowship with God? Are we deeply pained when circumstances interfere, and are we penitent

when we miss intimacy with God because of our own neglect? How necessary and important is friendship and fellowship with God? Is it our ever-increasing desire to live
with and for him? Sometimes the Lord tests us to arouse
or reawaken a compelling sense of need.

God's Loving Concern

But is God mindful of our longing; is he able and willing
to fulfill our desire? The psalmist need not doubt; he need
have no fear. When the Israelites were traveling through
the wilderness, a dry and weary land, the Lord their God
caused water to flow from a rock and opened streams in
the desert. Again, this saint with such deep desire in his soul
must have been aware of the prophet's pleading call, "Come,
all you who are thirsty, come to the waters . . ." (Isa. 55:1a).

God is never indifferent. He is able and eager to satisfy
not only our physical needs, but all the deep yearnings of
our spirit, and the earnest desires of our faith.

With what beauty and certainty that knowledge is revealed to us in Jesus Christ! We turn to a narrative found
in the seventh chapter of John's Gospel. It was the great
day of the Feast of Tabernacles. After living in huts and
temporary shelters for a week as a reminder of the ancestral
journey to the promised land, the people returned to Jerusalem and to their homes. During each day of that feast the
priests with golden vessels would draw water from the pool
of Siloam and offer it publicly in the temple as a libation.
During this time the multitude shouted, "With joy do we
draw water from the wells of salvation."

It was on that occasion that Jesus stood and cried, "If
any man is thirsty let him come to me and drink." Were the
people only observing a custom, simply going through the
motions, or was their action more than a ceremony? Let
each one in the throng search his soul and if he truly feels
a great need of salvation's peace and satisfaction let him

come to the man of Nazareth, the prophet of Galilee, the Son of God who alone is able to supply grace beyond measure.

The Emphatic Declaration

We are stirred by Jesus' tremendous claim. His language is so comprehensive, so universal, "If any man." No one in the multitude need fear frustration. Jesus will not fail; he will satisfy. Had he not in effect said the same thing to the Samaritan woman with whom he conversed at Jacob's well: "Everyone who drinks this water will be thirsty again, but whoever drinks the water I give him will never thirst" (John 4:13 – 14a).

And the promise is as astounding as the invitation, "Whosoever believes in me, as the Scripture has said, streams of living water will flow from within him" (John 7:38). The Son of God makes abundant provision. The fountain of mercy never runs dry; the river of grace is the greatest river in the world.

Two things are necessary to enjoy that fulness of grace: we must believe and we must exercise our faith. We must listen and obey. We must come and drink.

Those who are blessed become a blessing to others. They experience the blessing of receiving salvation and then the added privilege of giving, for as Jesus says, "streams of living water shall flow from within him." Then follows the elucidation: "By this he meant the Spirit, whom those who believed in him were later to receive" (John 7:39).

How wonderful! We no longer enjoy Christ's physical presence. He no longer walks the streets of our cities and towns, and we no longer hear his voice. But He is with us through his Spirit who dwells in our hearts, constantly supplying our need of grace and making us channels of mercy to those around us.

So today, as through all decades and centuries, the call is extended; "Whoever is thirsty, let him come; and whoever wishes, let him take the free gift of the water of life" (Rev. 22:17). Beautiful words of grace! This divine offer of salvation is found throughout Scripture and is reiterated at the very close.

The Required Response

Do you long for closer fellowship with God, for greater assurance that you are his child? Would you know the fulness of satisfaction and joy which only God can give? Then come to him, Yes, come again and again. Do not hesitate. "Any man," "whosoever," surely includes you and me. You can be sure, for the encouragement comes from God. His invitation is sincere; his promise is sure.

Here is the clear invitation:

Come where the fountain flows, river of life;
Healing for all thy woes, doubting and strife.
Millions have been supplied, no one was e'er denied
Come to the crimson tide; come, sinner, come.

                                                                 Henry Burton

Here is the believer's response:

I heard the voice of Jesus say,
"Behold, I freely give
The living water; thirsty one
Stoop down and drink and live."

I came to Jesus and I drank
Of that life-giving stream;
My thirst was quenched, my soul revived,
And now I live in Him.

                                                  Horatius Bonar, 1846

Here is the divine assurance: "Blessed are those who hunger and thirst for righteousness, for they will be filled" (Matt. 5:6).

6

Glorying in the Cross

May I never boast except in the cross of our Lord Jesus Christ, through which the world has been crucified to me, and I to the world (Gal. 6:14).

A. **The Boastful Sinner**
    1. Claiming righteousness according to the law
    2. Confronted with Christ, realizes sin
B. **The Imperfect Saint**
    1. Tempted to consider himself superior to others
    2. In need of divine correction
C. **The Joyful Proclamation**
    1. Because of its' divine character
    2. Because of its saving power
D. **The Wonderful Transformation**
    1. A new relationship to God
    2. A different relationship to the world

The Boastful Sinner

Let us admit it, by nature we are proud. All men are inclined to boast. And the apostle Paul was no exception.

There was a time in his life when he found great satisfaction in the thought of his superiority to others. He was a man of exceptional gifts and, trained in the school of the Pharisees as a student of the renowned teacher, Gamaliel,

Paul was thoroughly acquainted with the Law of God and tried to observe it with meticulous perfection. Preoccupied with the letter of the law, Paul was satisfied with external conformity and failed to see that he fell far short of its real demand: that he love God with all his heart, soul, mind, and strength. Paul was sure that he merited divine approbation; he rested hopes for such approval on his good works. He was self-righteous, an attitude which God detests and which the Bible condemns.

The commandments of God teach and enlighten. They are designed to impress us with God's holiness and our own depravity. The law is the mirror in which we see ourselves as we really are in the sight of God. It unmasks us, exposes our sin, and calls for penitent confession — not self-congratulation. Sinai should begin our journey to Calvary.

On the road to Damascus, the Lord stopped Paul in his tracks and brought him to his knees. Paul was made aware of his folly as a persecutor of Christ and the Church, and was made a member and a great leader in that church. The gospel he had hated now became the message he loved. He no longer boasted of his own goodness but gloried in the grace of God.

The Imperfect Saint

Could it be that Paul had something else in mind when he expressed his commitment to glory in nothing but the cross of Christ? That is not at all unlikely. In the early Christian church Paul had become the most prominent figure. He distinguished himself as both missionary and theologian. His zeal and performance was such that the church of all ages is indebted to him.

So now he faced another temptation. Compare his service and accomplishments in the work of the Lord with the limited performance of others and see how he surpassed

them. Like Saul, the first king of Israel, Paul stood head
and shoulders above his contemporaries. You may be certain that the devil tempted him to be proud. In fact he
himself confesses, "To keep me from becoming con-
ceited . . . , there was given me a thorn in the flesh, a messenger of Satan, to torment me" (2 Cor. 12:7).

The apostle was given a constant reminder that he must
glory in God's grace and not in his own good works. This
persistent, loving discipline bore fruit in the humble confession: "For I am the least of the apostles and do not
even deserve to be called an apostle, because I persecuted
the church of God. But by the grace of God I am what I
am . . ." (1 Cor. 15:9, 10a).

We can readily see the sin of pride in others, while we
often fail to see it in ourselves. You probably have heard of
the man who declared, "I am very grateful that I am so
humble."

If we are honest with ourselves, all of us discover a de-
gree of Pharisaism in our hearts. We take pride in our accomplishments, we point out our good deeds, we compare
ourselves with others to our own advantage. We are decent
and respectable. We are not delinquent as some others are
in church attendance and in gifts to God. Do we really
deserve applause? All that is truly good in our lives is the
fruit of God's grace and Spirit. But it is easy to consider
ourselves better than others and the idea of salvation by
works is the most persistent heresy in the history of the
Christian church.

With Paul we must learn to glory not in ourselves but in
the cross of Christ. That is evidence of genuine spiritual
transformation.

Consider what Paul is saying. He is speaking of the miracle of grace which made him "a new creature." Once he
hated the gospel, he persecuted the church, he despised the

cross, and considered Jesus of Nazareth a prevaricator and a blasphemer of God's Name.

But then the crucified Jesus confronted Paul and presented undeniable evidence of his resurrection. Paul saw and heard! He was convinced of the truth of the gospel and was convicted of his own stubbornness and spiritual blindness. That day Paul became a believer, called to be an apostle, a promoter of the truth he had so vehemently denied. He saw and experienced the wonder of God's grace. The cross became very precious to him; that he should glory in anything else would be sacrilege.

The Joyful Proclamation

Why did Paul glory in the cross? In light of what he has shared in his epistles the answer is loud and clear.

The cross is the revelation of God. It does not conflict with or abolish the law, rather it confirms all that the law declares by fulfilling its demands. The wonderful message of the gospel is that what we were supposed to do, but could not, God has done for us in Christ. The crucified Savior is a further unfolding of all that Moses and the prophets had declared. We glory in the cross because of its meaning and power.

Paul rejoiced in the cross because it brought about his personal salvation. How blind he had been to think that his works were meritorious, deserving of God's favor! How mortified he was by the recollection that he had attempted to work his way to heaven! What ignorance! What folly!

He could be saved in the only way that sinners have ever been or ever will be saved—by grace and by grace alone. Paul became a true child of God when he realized that Jesus had died for his sins. He prayed that he would never forget that fact and with God's help he never did. Listen to Paul's testimony: "I have been crucified with Christ and I no longer live, but Christ lives in me. The life I live in the body, I live by faith in the Son of God, who loved me and gave himself for me" (Gal. 2:20). In Christ Paul found forgiveness of sins and everlasting blessedness; the cross changed his whole life.

And Paul was surrounded by evidence of God's saving power as revealed in Christ who died to save sinners and gather to himself a church. Wherever the gospel was proclaimed, men and women, Jew and Gentile were saved.

To be sure, that gospel met with opposition. It was distorted, denied, scorned, and rejected by men. Paul himself said ". . . but we preach Christ crucified, a stumbling block to Jews and foolishness to Gentiles." And on that score attitudes toward the gospel have not changed. Proud of their self-sufficiency and achievements, men are still scandalized by the cross. It takes a miracle of grace to change their hearts.

But God's truth is universally victorious. In this conviction, bolstered by continued demonstration of the gospel's power, the apostle vowed that he would proclaim nothing but the crucified Christ. The gospel has many aspects which serve to underscore the riches of God's grace, but let us, as Christians, never forget the centrality of the cross.

The Wonderful Transformation

According to Paul, the cross is not only our message to others but the controlling influence in our own experience. Note what he says about it: ". . . by which the world has been crucified to me, and I to the world."

Shall we speak of a second crucifixion? We hesitate. Let us rather speak of the effect of Christ's sacrifice on our lives, and of its continuing influence on our daily behavior.

Our new relationship to God means an altogether different relationship to the world. Yet, we are still happy to sing: This is my Father's world; . . . I rest me in the thought. . . ."

Far be it from anyone of us to forget that we live in God's world, lest we fail to give him the praise and thanks which we owe him for all the bounties and beauties of the earth, and for all the blessings of life.

But there is another aspect, the one which Paul underscores in this text. This world is a sinful world opposed to God. All who are not allied with Christ are hostile to the gospel. By nature we are enemies of God destined to go down in horrible, final defeat unless our hearts are renewed and our lives are sanctified.

But thank God, believers have been provided victory in Christ. For them:

> The penalty of sin has been paid
> The power of sin is broken
> The presence of sin will be removed

We are no longer slaves to sin; we have been emancipated. We belong to Jesus who purchased us with his precious blood. Our Savior has become our Lord. The joy of salvation goes hand-in-hand with the joy of service. Our interest is no longer in sinful things, even though we are tempted by them, but our heart's desire is to be pleasing to God in all things.

Do we understand Paul's meaning and are we ready to follow his example — proclaiming and living the message of the cross?

A little boy, having come from the sanctuary where the sun had been shining brightly on the stained-glass windows, was asked in the Sunday school class what Christian life was. After a moment's thought, he smiled and replied, "A Christian is somebody who has the light shining through." Yes, we proclaim Christ to others by reflecting the light of his truth and grace. The message of the crucified Christ is revealed by fellowship with the living Christ.

In the cross of Christ I glory,
　　Tow'ring o'er the wrecks of time;
All the light of sacred story
　　Gathers round its head sublime.

When the woes of life o'er take me,
　　Hopes deceive and fears annoy,
Never shall the cross forsake me;
　　Lo! it glows with peace and joy.

Bane and blessing, pain and pleasure
　　By the cross are sanctified;
Peace is there that knows no measure,
　　Joys that through all time abide.
　　　　　　　　　　　John Bowring, 1825

7

The Savior's Parting Words

> *And he said to them, "I have eagerly desired to eat this Passover with you before I suffer. For I tell you, I shall not eat it again until it finds fulfillment in the kingdom of God"* (Luke 22:15, 16).

A. Words of Tender Concern
   1. His disciples are troubled
   2. This is the last Passover
B. Words of Intense Desire
   1. That faith may be strengthened
   2. That fellowship may be enjoyed
   3. That minds may be enlightened
C. Words of Impending Sorrow
   1. He is about to leave them
   2. He leaves by way of the cross
D. Words of Reassuring Hope
   1. He will return as their living Lord
   2. A glad and glorious reunion awaits
E. Words of Needed Encouragement
   1. For us when we are afraid
   2. The cross means victory

Words of Tender Concern

Where are the multitudes with which Jesus was commonly surrounded? Where is the throng that had come to Jerusalem to keep the Passover? Where are the carping critics who have sought to discredit him? They are not present in the upper room. This hour has been reserved for intimate fellowship with his disciples.

These are the men who have answered his call and with whom he has had a very special relationship during three years of public ministry. On more than one occasion he has taken them aside for private instruction. They have a prominent part in his prayers. He loves them more than they know, and, with the exception of Judas Iscariot, they have learned to love him too. Now that he is about to leave them, they will be deeply hurt. Parting from those who are dear is never easy.

Patiently and persistently Jesus had sought to prepare his disciples for this trying experience. He had openly predicted his death on the cross but it was a revelation they were unwilling to accept. Thomas had demurred and Peter had expressed bold opposition. The disciples simply could not accept the thought of such a horrible end to his life and ministry. And to the extent that they were unconvinced, they were unprepared.

Jesus had observed their troubled faces and understood the turmoil in their hearts. They were not ready to let him go and surely not in the manner he predicted. He does not berate them for their stubborn resistance; rather, he continues to encourage them to trusting acceptance.

He underscores the special significance of "this Passover." It is the final supper which he and his disciples will share, and is meant to sustain and strengthen their faith.

This meal will remind them of their forefathers' deliverance from Egypt. They escaped judgment by the sign of blood on the doorposts of their dwellings, they partook of food that they might be fortified for the journey they were about to begin. The disciples are reminded of God's saving grace and power.

The Passover was also a prophecy. Through many years and centuries it served as a promise of the greater deliver-

ance which was to come — deliverance from the bondage of
sin. That deliverance is at hand but it requires Jesus' death
on a cross.

You see Jesus' tender concern. His disciples' faith will be
tested to the limit, but as the mystery of the cross unfolds
they must view it in the light of divine providence and
promise. Though they will not understand, they must trust.
They must walk with God because only he can reveal the
grace and glory of his redemptive plan.

Words of Intense Desire

The disciples cherished every moment with Jesus and
longed for continued fellowship. Oh, that it would never
end! Jesus knows their feelings and now he reveals his own.
His love is greater; his longing is more intense than theirs.
Listen to what he says, "I have eagerly desired to eat this
passover with you. . . ." He has been anticipating this communion with earnest expectation.

Why? We cannot answer that question fully. If we have
difficulty understanding the profundity of his thoughts, how
could we expect to fathom the depth of his emotions?

But we are not left in complete ignorance. Jesus had
longed for this moment because of love to be shared, because of memories to cherish, because of the message from
heaven portrayed in this sacrament, and because it provided
occasion for him to shed light on the cross.

As the disciples partake of the sacramental feast they will
experience a great blessing. They will be in communion
with God's presence, hear his voice, and feast on his truth
and grace. They will be reminded that: "God works in a
mysterious way, His wonders to perform."

Yes, the Savior is filled with longing for fellowship together in God's appointed way, that the disciples may be
assured that God is indeed the God of salvation. He who

delivered their fathers will deliver them. They must look to God for he himself will set the example. Then their doubts will be removed, their fears allayed. "Seeing is believing?" No, it's the other way around; believing is seeing.

Words of Impending Sorrow

Jesus does not obscure the fact that he is going away. In unequivocal words he declares that this is his final observance of the Passover with his disciples. He is going away and will no longer walk and talk with them as heretofore. This is the night of farewell. Once again he points to the manner of his departure as he underscores the fact that he is about to suffer.

To be sure he has already suffered much: Nazareth had turned against him, Capernaum and other cities had refused to believe, and Jerusalem had not responded to his pleading call. His message was derided and his person is to be attacked. Even now the leaders of the people were plotting against him in the hope of bringing about his defeat. Jesus knew pain and sorrow.

But now the time of crisis has arrived, the climactic hour of his supreme sacrifice. He will be scourged and beaten, mocked and scorned, condemned and crucified. Forces of earth and hell will unleash their hateful and dreaded power. With thorn-crowned brow and nail-pierced hands he will shed his blood. And he will cry out "I thirst," and in bitter agony of spirit will utter the astonishing, incomprehensible lament, "My God, my God, why hast thou forsaken me?"

The words of the prophet Isaiah are about to be fulfilled: He was despised and rejected by men; a man of sorrows . . . stricken by God . . . pierced for our transgressions . . . crushed for our iniquities (Isa. 53:3 – 5).

But the consolation in Jesus' prediction of his impending suffering is the awareness he shares with his disciples that

the cross is not a surprise. It is not an unexpected turn of
events, but is essential to the program of redemption. It has
a glorious purpose, necessary in the Father's plan. He accepted the suffering and would endure it in perfect obedience and submission.

This plan is beyond the disciples' comprehension. They
do not have his insight. To them the cross can appear only
to be a tragedy, a terrible mistake. They will be shocked
and horrified, but they must find help and consolation in
the knowledge that though Jesus foresaw the cross on the
road ahead, that is the way he chose to go. They must trust
him; they must trust God. When they see that in reality
Christ's cross is their cross, that he suffered and died in
their stead, they will recognize that this terrible display of
wrath is concurrently the most glorious demonstration of
divine love. They will discover the meaning of his words,
"Greater love has no man than this. . . . The good shepherd
lays down his life for the sheep" (John 15:13a; 10:11b).

Words of Reassuring Hope

When Jesus told his disciples that he would suffer and
die, he reminded them in the same breath that he would
rise again on the third day. But in their sadness they failed
to appropriate that comfort.

Now he reiterates that note of cheer and victory. This is
his last Passover with them on earth, but he assures them
that it is not the last for all time to come. We hear him say,
"I shall not eat it again until it finds fulfilment in the kingdom of God." The meaning is clear: though about to die,
he will live again; and though the time of parting has come,
it is only temporary. A glad reunion awaits. The crucified
Savior will return to them as their living Lord.

In the cross there is promise of a crown. The Passover
they have commemorated and the Lord's Supper they will

celebrate are prefigurations of that great heavenly feast where they shall enjoy with him a fellowship that knows no bounds and that shall never end. They shall see him face to face, and shall be changed into his likeness.

Believers in Christ must look to the cross and then beyond the cross to understand its glorious meaning. The heart of their theology and the theme of their song is and will ever be: Saved by the blood of the Lamb.

Words of Needed Encouragement

The words Jesus addressed to his disciples have wonderful meaning for us.

Sometimes we are vexed by doubt: Is the gospel really true?

Sometimes our faith is tested when we are derided for the foolishness of our confession. How can anybody be saved by the blood of the cross?

Sometimes we are concerned about the genuineness of our own faith. We ask: Am I really a child of God?

Sometimes we hesitate to come to the Lord's Table. Are we worthy?

Jesus understands our plight and so he calls us to renew our faith. We are invited to put all our faith in him who died to save us and who now lives to complete his saving work in us. Jesus calls, he beckons, he reaches down to help us. He will bring us safely to our heavenly home.

Calvary spells victory:

Victory for God as he reclaims a lost and sinful world.
Victory for Christ who conquered sin and death.
Victory for sinners for whom he paid the penalty.
Victory for saints for whom he opened the ever-flowing
     fountain of mercy.

Saints of God, rejoice in the Lord.

8

The Lord's Supper

For I have received from the Lord what I also passed on to you: The Lord Jesus, on the night he was betrayed, took bread, and when he had given thanks, he broke it and said, "This is my body, which is for you; do this in remembrance of me." In the same way, after supper he took the cup, saying, "This cup is the new covenant in my blood: do this whenever you drink it, in remembrance of me." For whenever you eat this bread and drink this cup, you proclaim the Lord's death until he comes (1 Cor. 11:23 – 26).

A. A Striking Memorial
B. A Blessed Fellowship
C. A Promised Grace
D. A Holy Sacrament
E. A Believing Participation
F. A Clear Proclamation
G. A Glorious Hope

Y ou have heard children sing, "Count your many blessings, name them one by one." This is impossible because God's favors are more than we can number, greater than we can measure. With Moses we exclaim, "Who is like you, a people saved by the Lord?" (Deut. 33:29). God is incomparable and his people are special, his grace is infinite.

As we again commemorate our Savior's death on the

48

cross it is well that we reflect on the significance of the Lord's Supper. Briefly we dwell on seven aspects of the precious meaning and message it holds for us. May such thoughtful meditation lead to a rich spiritual blessing.

A Striking Memorial

The gospel writers tell us that the Lord's Supper was instituted by Christ himself. He is the one who broke the bread, poured out the wine, and instructed his disciples, "This do." Of this, Paul gives us a clear reminder when he says, "For I received of the Lord what I also passed on to you," whereupon he reviews what Jesus did in the upper room during his last night on earth.

The memorial to Christ's ministry on earth is not a towering statue, an extensive library, a beautiful park, or an avenue named in his honor. That is what men do. But Christ provides a simple supper of broken bread and poured wine, symbols of his death on the cross, as a reminder of what he did for our salvation.

"This do!" That is his command. Deserving of all our adoration and praise, he asks that we cling to him in humble faith, remembering him as the One who gave his life on Calvary's cross that we might receive forgiveness of sins and eternal life. The symbol of the Christian faith is the cross; and the Lord's Supper is a holy memorial telling us to keep looking to Christ crucified for comfort and assurance.

A Blessed Fellowship

We speak of the Lord's Supper as Holy Communion. Such it was meant to be and such it is: holy and blessed fellowship with God and his people.

Communion with God! We come to God in that new

and living way which he himself has opened for us in Christ. At the Lord's Table we are guests. How badly we need this intimate fellowship and how greatly the Lord himself delights in it! The God of all grace is pleased when his children are filled and refreshed with the bounties of his goodness, and they in turn rejoice and give thanks.

Communion with God's people! The feast is served family style. Fellow believers, members of the family of God, gather together at the Lord's Table to express their love for one another, and to be strengthened in that love. In communion with God they enjoy the blessed fellowship of the saints rejoicing in the fact that God saves individuals and that the individuals are in a church — one in faith, in hope, in love, one in the Lord!

A Promised Grace

We are mindful of the warning issued: "For anyone who eats and drinks without recognizing the body of the Lord eats and drinks judgment on himself" (1 Cor. 11:29). We are warned of judgment and condemnation.

But think of the positive side! Bread and wine are provided as symbols of Christ who is heavenly bread for the hungry and living water for the thirsty. Partaking of the Lord's Supper in faith, our souls are nourished and refreshed as we experience the sufficiency of God's grace and are promised that God will continue to satisfy every need.

> Come, for the feast is spread, hark to the call;
> Come to the living bread, offered to all. . . .
> Come, where the fountain flows, river of life,
> Healing for all thy woes, doubting and strife. . . .
> Whate'er thy want may be
> Here is the grace for thee
> Jesus thine only plea; come, Christian come.
>   Henry Burton

A Holy Sacrament

The Lord's Supper is not a sacrifice but a sacrament which points us to the greatest sacrifice ever made. Remember, Jesus broke the bread and poured out the wine. He did so as an indication that his body would be broken and his blood would be shed in perfect atonement for our sins.

Jesus' disciples, and early Christians as well, were well-acquainted with sacrifices. No one understood their meaning better than Jesus himself. He knew that they portrayed the perfect Lamb of God whose blood alone could reconcile men and God. He was well aware that he was that Lamb and also the great High Priest who would offer himself on the sacrificial altar—the cross.

An eyewitness to that sacrifice, the apostle Peter, has expressed it perfectly, "For you know that it was not with perishable things such as silver or gold that you were redeemed . . . but with the precious blood of Christ, a lamb without blemish or defect" (1 Peter 1:18, 19).

A Believing Participation

We are not present at the Lord's Supper as spectators. No, we eat and drink in participation. We do so in faith, believing that as surely as we eat the bread and drink the wine, so surely our sins are forgiven us for Christ's sake.

In a sense all of life is a confession. By word, deed, attitude, and action we manifest who we are. That is surely true at the Lord's Table. There we confess our faith in the God of our salvation—the Father who planned it, the Son who purchased it, and the Spirit who applies it.

Devout participation requires preparation. If even the holy exercise of prayer can become routine, partaking of the Lord's Supper can also be matter-of-fact, a mere custom rather than sheer delight, holy communion, a foretaste of heaven. We must come in true faith and with longing hearts.

A Clear Proclamation

Jesus says, "This do in remembrance of me." Says the apostle, ". . . you proclaim the Lord's death." Christians are not ashamed of the cross; they glory in it. That cruel instrument of torture, that shameful act of sinful men, is the supreme revelation of love divine. The cross spells salvation which is the central theme of God's word.

Can you think of a more beautiful and gracious heavenly message than this: "But God demonstrates his own love for us in this: While we were still sinners, Christ died for us" (Romans 5:8)?

If that is what God revealed and if that is our confession, then let it be our proclamation. Let us tell what we have heard so that a world in need may hear a message of hope and deliverance, and that Jesus the Savior of men may be magnified as sinners are led to the way of salvation and as saints follow him.

A Glorious Hope

Jesus promised that some day his followers would sit with him at the great feast, the marriage supper of the Lamb. The apostle reminds us that we are to proclaim the Lord's death "until he comes." Yes, the crucified Savior is our living Lord.

He is coming again, we know not just when. But it will happen as surely as God is God, and as surely as the promises of God are true.

We look forward to that day; a day of defeat for all the enemies of Christ, a day of victory for all his followers. Everywhere, and at all times, send forth the message that

Jesus saves. That is the sinner's only hope and the believer's only comfort. May the Lord's Supper inspire us to tell the good news, the best news this world has ever heard. Let us tell what we have seen and heard, and what we know to be wonderfully true. When you leave the Lord's table may it be with a firm resolve and conviction that in some way, be it ever so small, you will prepare yourself and others for the return of Christ.

9

In Remembrance

Do this in remembrance of me (1 Cor. 11:24b).

A. **Communion with the Disciples**
  1. In the upper room
  2. The night of farewell
  3. Jesus points to the cross
  4. With amazing self-forgetfulness
  5. To prepare his disciples
B. **Focusing on the Cross**
  1. Lest they forget
  2. That divine grace may be magnified
  3. That believers may be sanctified
C. **Believing Participation**
  1. Observing the Lord's Supper
    a) Surely a duty
    b) Unquestionably a privilege
  2. Remembering Christ's sacrifice
    a) To learn the meaning of the gospel
    b) To enjoy the comfort of the gospel

Communion with the Disciples

As the gospel writers, Matthew, Mark, Luke, and John had done before him, so now the apostle Paul takes us to the scene in that upper room at Jerusalem where Jesus is gathered with his disciples during his last night on earth.

54

The door is held ajar. We must not intrude for this is holy ground, but we do pause to look and listen. The atmosphere is quiet, yet tense.

We glance at those present, recognizing the Twelve who have spent so much time with Jesus and who have come to know him well, with one exception. But not well enough. They still have much to learn.

During the closing weeks of his ministry Jesus has clearly revealed that he must suffer and die. His disciples failed to understand, they even demurred, but the master had "steadfastly set his face toward Jerusalem" and had even walked before them on the way. Jesus is undeterred and determined. He has an appointment to keep. He has a rendezvous with God; he must go to Calvary.

The hour has come. He has chosen to separate himself from the multitudes and from the leaders of the people who oppose him, that he may spend these private moments with his disciples. They are very special.

True, one of them has plotted against him and will be exposed as a traitor, but the others have need of enlightenment and reassurance. In just a little while he will leave this room and make his way to Gethsemane. If he is prepared, his disciples are not. They do not understand.

To be sure Old Testament revelation with which they are acquainted has pointed to the ordeal that awaits Jesus, but passages such as Psalm 22 and Isaiah 53 have been largely ignored. Jesus' own predictions have not registered. Pending developments will take the disciples by surprise; they will be baffled and horrified. In fact, we ask ourselves if Jesus himself was not staggered by increasing realization of the extent to which he must suffer so that he prays, "Father, if possible let this cup pass from me. But not my will, thine be done"? He faces condemnation by both God and men. He must endure excruciating pain, terrible shame, and incomprehensible accursedness.

It would be natural to assume that Jesus would be think-ing only of himself. All his life he has been concerned about others but surely in the present circumstances he will be preoccupied with the crisis he himself faces. The night is dark; the way is difficult; there is no one to help. But he must proceed, until he finds himself alone, terribly alone. Where he goes his disciples cannot come. He and he alone must bear the burden of God's wrath against sin.

Was Jesus discouraged? He had proclaimed the gospel in word and deed but his warnings had gone unheeded and his invitations unaccepted. Only a few had taken the mes-sage to heart. It is to them that he turns in this final hour. He is concerned about their ordeal even though his own is far greater. With amazing self-forgetfulness he ministers to their needs. As he does so, we listen.

Focusing on the Cross

What does he say? He breaks bread and pours out wine and, inviting the Twelve to partake, he says, "Do this in remembrance of Me." What profound import in those sim-ple words! He points his disciples to the cross and tells them they must never, never forget their destination.

Are these disciples, and many more who will join them during the course of history, in danger of forgetting? How tragic but nevertheless true! God's people had been given the Passover as a reminder of their deliverance from Egypt, a memorial had been raised to commemorate their miracu-lous crossing of the Jordan as they entered the "promised land." Yet the Book of Deuteronomy is filled from begin-ning to end with the admonition that they must remember the Lord their God and all that he had done. Too often such words go unheeded. Our memory and faith are so imperfect and spiritual values are often obscured by our interest in physical and material things. We fail to keep proper balance. Our attention is diverted.

In this appointment of the Lord's Supper as the memorial of his sacrifice on the cross, Jesus asserts that the grace of God shall be magnified and the name of God shall be glorified. Calvary is not an admission of defeat but a proclamation of victory. It marks the victory of God's grace, a fulfillment of God's redemptive plan. If we view it with sorrow because of our guilty involvement, we view it with joy because of the outpouring of divine love. Hear once again the supremely beautiful summary of the gospel: "For God so loved the world that he gave his one and only Son, that whoever believes in him shall not perish but have eternal life" (John 3:16).

But if the Lord's Supper has been given us that God may be praised, it also has as a primary purpose that we may be assured of our salvation. In this sign and seal of God's promises, we are given confidence that all our sins are forgiven. We are reconciled to God: As members in Christ we will never be subjected to the punishment for sin which Christ endured on our behalf. We are God's own dear children and as such we are heirs of eternal life.

Ask yourself: Who is it that is troubled by sin? The unbeliever is unconcerned. He needs to be awakened to an awareness of evil in his own heart and life. But those who believe and who have fellowship with God develop ever-increasing sensitivity to their lack of conformity to his holy demands. They are troubled by the fact of sin, not only the sins of others, but also their own. This must not rob them of comfort. He who forgives our sin will also cleanse us from it. Of this we may be sure for he tells us in his word: "If we walk in the light, as he is in the light, we have fellowship with one another, and the blood of Jesus, his Son, purifies us from every sin. . . . If we confess our sins, he is faithful and just and will forgive us our sins and purify us from all unrighteousness" (1 John 1:7–9).

What the word teaches, the sacrament confirms. We are not sinless and perfect in ourselves, but in Jesus, God's Son, our Lord, we are right with God. The chasm has been bridged, the barriers are removed not by our own efforts but by grace divine.

> My sin — O the bliss of this glorious thought! —
> My sin, not in part, but the whole,
> Is nailed to the cross and I bear it no more;
> Praise the Lord, praise the Lord, O my soul.
> > Horatio G. Spafford

These words of praise should be accompanied by the pleading prayer: "Wash away all my iniquity and cleanse me from my sin" (Ps. 51:2).

Believing Participation

Jesus said, "Do this" by which he clearly indicated that we are to eat the bread and drink the wine.

Was that a command? Without a doubt. To ignore or neglect the Lord's Supper is an act of disobedience. It is our duty to confess both our sin and our faith by believing participation. By admitting our need, we declare that Jesus has fulfilled that need.

We hasten to add that Jesus' words are more than a command. They constitute a kindly instruction and a gracious invitation. In the upper room, on this first occasion of this sacred observance the disciples do not realize the full and blessed implications of the act in which they engage. Jesus is still preparing them for the cross; he has not yet been crucified. He realizes that they cannot grasp the truly amazing significance of what he is about to accomplish on this great day of atonement which has now arrived.

But this night will end and the morrow will present a

graphic demonstration of what is meant by the broken bread and the poured out wine. The disciples will see the cross in all its grim reality. Through succeeding years they will not be able to forget that scene. And they must not. For there is glory in that shame; mercy in that judgment. The Savior's death means life for sinners like you and me. Always and again we must look to Jesus. He is our salvation. What a privilege to know and to remember him!

And so, in glad obedience we, along with all believers and the Christian church, observe the Lord's Supper in commemoration of Jesus' death on the cross. We have received much fuller and clearer revelation than the disciples had when they were gathered that night in the upper room. They had much to learn and so have we. But this we know: Jesus, the great high priest, has offered himself as the Lamb of God on the altar of Calvary's cross that all who believe in him may be saved. This is the gospel. This is the message the Lord's Supper affirms. We listen and believe, for the voice we hear is the voice of God.

I urge you to appropriate the fullness of the promised blessing. Here at the Lord's Table is the grace you need.

Come, confessing your need of forgiveness and grace.

Come, seeking the blessing God so graciously offers.

Come, enjoying the fellowship with fellow members of God's family.

Come, rejoicing in and praising the God of your salvation.

And having come, renew your vow to come again.

> According to thy gracious word,
>   In meek humility,
> This will I do, my dying Lord,
>   I will remember thee.

Thy body, broken for my sake,
My bread from heaven shall be;
The testamental cup I take,
And thus remember thee.
                James Montgomery

Only then, can we live in remembrance of him, devoting each day of our lives to service and praise for our Lord.

10

The Wondrous Cross

. . . and the Lord has laid on him the iniquity of us all (Isa. 53:6).

A. The Supreme Revelation
   1. From the God of salvation
   2. The divine answer to the sin problem
   3. Its clarity and certainty
B. The Great Transferral
   1. Repeatedly recognized
   2. Considering Messiah's glory and humiliation
   3. Jesus, the scapegoat
   4. Revealing infinite love
C. The Staggering Burden
   1. Beyond comprehension
   2. Marvelously inclusive
   3. Bringing blessed relief

When Jesus came into this world he came to die. His death on the cross was the appointed and necessary sacrifice for the salvation of sinners. The Bible refers to him as "the Lamb that was slain from the creation of the world" (Rev. 13:8). And so after thirty-three years on earth, in the very prime of life, having observed the law and having proclaimed the gospel in word and deed, he suffered and died on the cross of Calvary.

The thought of death makes us uncomfortable. We were created to live, not to die. Our natural inclination is to turn away from death in any form, surely a crucifixion. Others died in similar fashion, but we hasten to add that the death of Christ was unique. It was the greatest injustice ever committed. Jesus, the Son of God, suffered at the hands of God and men. He endured the agonies of earth and hell. Who can fathom the meaning of the words: "God made him who knew no sin to be sin [sin-offering] for us" (2 Cor. 5:21)?

But when we view the cross in the light of God's word, when we see it with the eyes of faith, we behold the beauty and wonder of the cross. If it demonstrates the wrath of God against sin, it also proclaims God's love for sinners. It is the supreme revelation of his truth and grace.

It is for that reason that we testify in the words of the poet James Allen:

> Sweet the moments, rich in blessing
> Which before the cross we spend,
> Life, and health, and peace possessing,
> From the sinner's dying Friend.
>
> Here I rest, in wonder viewing
> All my sins on Jesus laid,
> Here I see redemption flowing
> From the sacrifice he made.
>
> Here I find the dawn of heaven
> While upon the cross I gaze
> See my trespasses forgiven,
> And my songs of triumph raise.

The Supreme Revelation

Long before it happened, Isaiah had a vision of the Savior's purpose. In his prophecy Isaiah castigates men for their sinful ways; he warns of judgment to come and issues a pleading, persistent call to repentance. Unswervingly he proclaims the good news that God will bring salvation. God will provide the answer to the most vexing problem in all the world and in the life of every individual — the problem of sin.

Isaiah speaks of the Lord, the God of almighty power who is the covenant God of Israel in the Old Testament and of the church and all believers in the New Testament. He is the God of salvation which is his work from beginning to end. He planned it, he reveals it, he works it out and will bring it to perfect completion. And central to that plan, at the very heart of the gospel, is the cross.

We cannot possibly extricate ourselves from our entanglement in sin and misery; we can find no way to escape from judgment and condemnation.

Let us confess it. In sin we face:

> A question we cannot answer.
> A problem we cannot solve.
> A burden we cannot bear.
> A battle we cannot win.
> A price we cannot pay.

God saw our plight and recognized our hopeless condition, so he came to our rescue with the answer, the solution, the relief, the victory, and the sacrifice. The good news which Isaiah announced, and which has since been more fully revealed to us, is this: The Lord, creator of heaven and earth, whose power is limitless, is the God of all grace. He is our deliverer, our strength, and our consolation.

He refuses to relinquish his hold on the world and its inhabitants. His world shall be reclaimed and wandering sheep shall be brought back to the fold. His promises are sure and his faithfulness never dies.

Isaiah could see things to come with clarity and certainty

because he had a faithful understanding of God's love for his people. Coming events were revealed as if they had already happened. How tragic that many of his contemporaries did not understand and that succeeding generations forgot! Even those who looked and longed for a Messiah never expected a cross. They developed a blind spot to the Suffering Servant of the Lord.

If such neglect and misunderstanding was culpable, how much greater is our responsibility in the light of fuller and clearer revelation given us! The cross became reality. It was planted. There it stands in the midst of human history, a warning to those who give it no heed, a blessing to those who recognize it as the supreme revelation of God's grace.

The Great Transferral

I like the way the late Monseigneur Fulton J. Sheen began his autobiography by declaring that his life's story really began more than nineteen hundred years ago when Christ died for sinners on Calvary's cross. Christ's death brings life.

This truth has been stated even more eloquently by the apostle Paul: "I have been crucified with Christ and I no longer live, but Christ lives in me. The life I live in the body, I live by faith in the Son of God, who loved me and gave himself for me (Gal. 2:20).

But no one has ever expressed it more simply and beautifully than Jesus himself, "I am the good shepherd. The good shepherd lays down his life for the sheep" (John 10:11).

Now can we understand the great transferral of which Isaiah speaks when he declares, "the Lord has laid on him the iniquity of us all"? We must go back to the prophet's own words as he first of all portrays the glory of the Messiah and then describes his humiliation. Contrast these two passages found in his prophecy:

> For to us a child is born,
>   to us a son is given,
>   and the government will be on his shoulders.
> And he will be called
>   Wonderful Counselor, Mighty God,
>   Everlasting Father, Prince of Peace. (Isa. 9:6)

> He was despised and rejected by men,
>   a man of sorrows, and familiar with suffering.
> Like one from whom men hide their faces
>   he was despised, and we esteemed him not.
> Surely he took up our infirmities
>   and carried our sorrows,
> Yet we considered him stricken by God
>   smitten by him and afflicted.
> But he was pierced for our transgressions,
>   he was crushed for our iniquities;
> the punishment that brought us peace was upon him,
>   and by his wounds we are healed. (Isa. 53:3 – 5)

That message must be understood in the light of the symbolism emphasized on the Great Day of Atonement as described in Leviticus where Aaron the High Priest is instructed:

Then he is to take the two goats and present them before the Lord at the entrance to the Tent of Meeting. He is to cast lots for the two goats — one lot for the Lord and the other for the scapegoat. Aaron shall bring the goat whose lot falls to the Lord and sacrifice it for a sin offering. But the goat chosen by lot as the scapegoat shall be presented alive before the Lord to be used for making atonement by sending it into the desert as a scapegoat. (Lev. 16:7 – 10)

We begin to comprehend what Isaiah meant when he said, "the Lord has laid on him the iniquity of us all." On the final Great Day of Atonement no lot was cast. Jesus was the appointed sacrifice. He was our substitute who died for our sin and he became the scapegoat to bear our sins away that we might be free. He was not sent into the wilderness but into the darkness of hell.

Have you ever heard of such love? Here it is in the gospel, the good news, "the greatest story ever told." God the Father transferred the burden of our sin and guilt to his Son Jesus Christ who bore condemnation, shame, and agony in our stead that we might be reconciled to God. He died that we might live.

The Staggering Burden

Can anyone really comprehend what Jesus did for us? He not only kept the law and offered obedience on our behalf, he also endured the penalty of the law and suffered our condemnation. He bore the burden of God's wrath against sin under which we should have perished everlastingly. The Son of God did what no one else could do. He died our death. He brought the required sacrifice which we ourselves could never bring.

And the burden Jesus bore was not the sin of just a few but, says Isaiah, "of us all." This is his believing confession: that Christ died for "his own" that they might be saved, healed, and made forever whole. Not one of them shall perish.

Would you know how many that includes? Did not Jesus command that the gospel should be preached throughout the world and did he not promise that men would come from far and near? In fact when he spoke of the cross he said, "But I, when I am lifted up from the earth, will draw all men to myself" (John 12:32).

That magnetism of the cross is being demonstrated every day in all areas of the earth. Yet, you and I shall continue to underestimate its appeal and power until we enjoy the

panoramic view given to the apostle John when exiled on
the isle of Patmos:

> After this I looked and there before me was a great mul-
> titude that no one could count, from every nation, tribe,
> people and language, standing before the throne and in
> front of the Lamb. They were wearing white robes and
> were holding palm branches in their hands. And they cried
> out in a loud voice: "Salvation belongs to our God, who
> sits on the throne, and to the Lamb" (Rev. 7:9 – 10).

As you sit at the Lord's Table commemorating Christ's
death on the cross, hang your head in shame because it was
your sins that nailed him to the tree. And then lift your
heart in praise at this wondrous cross where Christ died for
your salvation.

Not what my hands have done
Can save my guilty soul;
Not what my toiling flesh has borne
Can make my spirit whole.
Not what I feel or do
Can give me peace with God;
Not all my prayers and sighs and tears
Can bear my awful load.

Thy grace alone, O God,
To me can pardon speak;
Thy power alone, O Son of God,
Can this sore bondage break.
No other work save thine,
No other blood will do;
No strength save that which is divine
Can bear me safely through.

Horatius Bonar, 1864

11

Let Us Draw Near

Therefore, brothers, since we have confidence to enter the Most Holy Place by the blood of Christ ... and since we have a great priest over the house of God, let us draw near to God with a sincere heart in full assurance of faith ... (Heb. 10:19, 21, 22).

A. The Pastoral Admonition
  1. Draw near for fellowship
    a) Indispensable for spiritual joy and growth
    b) Illustrated in saints and in Jesus himself
  2. We must heed his call to communion
B. The Essential Requirement
  1. In God's way
  2. In faith
  3. With a sincere heart
  4. In full assurance
C. The Blessed Encouragement
  1. Jesus, our great High Priest
  2. Who has opened the way through his sacrifice
  3. Who is engaged in a heavenly ministry for us

The Pastoral Admonition

The author of the Epistle to the Hebrews, whoever he may have been, was a man of profound theological insight and a warm pastoral heart. He presents basic doctrinal insights but applies them in such a way that they become food for the soul and a guide for daily living.

As pilgrims and strangers on the earth, believers are making the greatest journey — the journey of life itself. In a world hostile to their beliefs and practices, they need one another. How blessed are they who need not walk alone but who have friends and relatives to provide the fellowship of love! More wonderful still is the spiritual communion which is ours as members of the family of God. We share our joys and bear one another's burdens.

But more than all, we need an intimate relationship with God. Having faith in God, we must exercise that faith in all that we do. As Christians we must live the Christian life. That which is usually considered secular must be permeated with spirituality. Then we walk with God, finding fulfilment and satisfaction in his service.

To live in that fashion requires moments of withdrawal, hours of quiet reflection, and joyful worship. In order to give ourselves to God, we must constantly receive. We are dependent on him for both salvation and service. Jesus reminded us of that when he said, "apart from me you can do nothing" (John 15:5). Indeed it is very necessary that we draw near to God.

Is this ardent devotion to God what characterized the lives of the greatest saints? Think of Abraham who constantly returned to the oaks of Mamre where he had built an altar to the Lord.

Think of Moses who enjoyed such intimate fellowship with God that his shining face reflected heavenly joy and peace.

Think of David who expressed the heart's deep longing:

> One thing I ask of the Lord
>   this is what I seek:
> that I may dwell in the house of the Lord
>   all the days of my life,
> to gaze upon the beauty of the Lord
>   and to seek him in his temple. (Ps. 27:4)

Think of Hannah (1 Sam. 1 – 2) who poured out her soul in pleading prayer and, when God heard, did not forget to bring him thanksgiving and praise.

Think of Paul, who directed fervent prayers for himself and the church "to him who is able to do immeasurably more than all we ask or imagine . . ." (Eph. 3:20).

And think of Jesus who "on the Sabbath day went in to the synagogue, as was his custom", (Luke 4:16), and who frequently separated himself from the multitudes for much-needed and treasured fellowship with his Father in heaven. His prayer life was exemplary because his faith was perfect and his burden was great. His life was one of communion with God. The Father was in him and he in the Father. But as the man from Nazareth, the prophet of Galilee, the Savior of sinners, he drew near to God again and again that while he walked the sands of time his heart might be in heaven. Fellowship with the Father was his supreme delight and doing the Father's will was his desire.

Shall we respond to the call, heed the admonition, and draw near to God, approaching "the throne of grace with confidence, so that we may receive mercy and find grace to help in our time of need" (Heb. 4:16)?

We come to the Lord's Table with fellow believers, and we are happy to be in communion with each other. We rejoice together in the fact that God is present in a very special way. That is his promise and that togetherness with one another and with God brings peace to our souls.

The Essential Requirement

When we draw near to God we must do so in his way, not our own. It is possible to observe the Lord's Supper in purely a formal way, as a matter of custom, but that does not bring blessing. It brings only disappointment; we are as sheep unfed and our souls are not satisfied.

What then must characterize our presence and participation? Remembering that the Lord's Supper is for believers, we must come as believers. That means we must come as sinners claiming no merit of our own but confessing Jesus as our only hope and plea. By faith we respond to the invitation extended and claim the promises given.

Understand the stipulation that we must draw near to God "with a sincere heart." God is not deceived. He knows our thoughts and desires. If we are not sincere in our acknowledgment of our sin and in our profession of faith, we shall not receive a blessing. In fact, the Bible emphatically declares that all who eat the bread and drink the wine of the sacrament in a superficial manner "eat and drink judgment to themselves." They increase their condemnation.

The Bible cites many instances of individuals who pretended piety and devotion, but their confession was without commitment. It is possible, we know, to be religious without being truly Christian or, as Paul expresses it to Timothy, "having a form of godliness but denying its power" (2 Tim. 3:5).

Surely it is necessary for us to be reminded of the necessity that we come to the Lord in all sincerity. Too easily religious exercise becomes routine. Our heart is not in it.

When we seek fellowship with God by reading his word, we must listen to his voice and concentrate on his message. We must:

Read it through

Study it well

Pray it in

Live it out, Only then can we

Pass it on

When we pray, which is fellowship supreme, we must:

Offer sincere confession.

Offer earnest petition.

Offer genuine thanksgiving.

When we come to the Lord's Supper, we must:

Understand its meaning.

Express our need.

Seek and appropriate its blessing.

Sorrow because of our sin.

Rejoice in our salvation.

Then we can come as we should, "in full assurance of faith." Looking at ourselves, we would not dare to come for we are sinners. But believing the message of the gospel as expressed in God's word and confirmed by the holy sacrament of the Lord's Supper, we know that we have been saved and that we are children of God. By eating the bread and drinking the wine in faith we have assurance that our fears and doubts are conquered.

The Blessed Encouragement

This encouragement is ours because Jesus Christ is our great high priest. In the Old Testament the priesthood of Aaron was succeeded by the Levitical priesthood. These priests served a wonderful purpose but they were limited and temporary. They were prophetic of the perfect high priest, Jesus, the Son of God, our Savior.

In the Old Testament the high priest entered the Holy of Holies once a year, on the Great Day of Atonement, to sprinkle blood on the mercy seat. That was symbolic. It has found fulfillment in Christ. He shed his blood as the perfect and complete sacrifice and has ascended to the Holy of Holies in heaven where his blood has been accepted as full atonement for our sins.

That is why the veil in the temple was torn from top to bottom at the time of his death. He has opened the "new and living way for us." Through him we have access to God and when we come in his name and on the basis of his sacrifice, we have assurance of divine grace and blessing. We are confident that our sins are forgiven and that God welcomes us as his own dear children.

What is more, even now our heavenly high priest is active on our behalf. He presents his sacrifice and also his prayers for our benefit. The author of this epistle states it so beautifully, "Therefore he is able to save completely those who come to God through him, because he always lives to intercede for them" (Heb. 7:25). He will finish the work which he has begun. Eternal redemption is assured. Saved, we are being sanctified. Sanctified, we shall be glorified.

Picture it this way. As we draw near to God in faith, Jesus comes to meet us and leads us to the Father's throne as those whom he purchased with his blood. Therefore have no fear.

Christ's sacrifice on the cross, now presented in heaven, is our encouragement. Our present and eternal salvation is never in doubt. Martha Snell Nicholson has said it so well:

My Advocate

I sinned, and straightway, posthaste, Satan flew
Before the presence of the most High God,
And made a railing accusation there.
He said, "This soul, this thing of clay and sod,
Has sinned, 'Tis true that he has named Thy Name,
But I demand his death, for Thou has said,

'The soul that sinneth, it shall die.' Shall not
Thy sentence be fulfilled? Is justice dead?
Send now this wretched sinner to his doom.
What other thing can righteous ruler Do?"
And thus he did accuse me day and night,
And every word he spoke, oh, God, was true!
Then quickly one rose up from God's right hand,
Before whose glory angels veiled their eyes,
He spoke, "Each jot and tittle of the law
Must be fulfilled; the guilty sinner dies!
But wait—suppose his guilt were all transferred
To Me, and that I paid the penalty!
Behold My hands, My Side, My feet! One day
I was made sin for him, and died that he
Might be presented faultless, at Thy throne!"
And Satan fled away. Full well he knew
That he could not prevail against such love,
For every word my dear Lord spoke was true.

Let us draw near to God in Jesus' name and we shall be
blessed for his sake.

12

The Supreme Confession

Whoever acknowledges me before men, I will acknowledge him before my Father in heaven (Matt. 10:32).

A. Its Urgency
1. For those who:
    a) Have received abundant revelation
    b) Claim to be God's children
    c) Know Jesus' personal ministry
    d) Are concerned about the world's desperate need
2. How can we be indifferent!
B. Its Nature
1. A positive requirement
2. The central theme
3. The all-embracing area
C. Its Reward
1. Christ identifies at his ascension
2. He intercedes for us at the Father's throne
3. He will claim and glorify us at his return

Your life is not a secret. To be sure it has very personal and private aspects so that there are many things about us that others do not know, need not know, and should not know. On the other hand, in what we do and say, we are constantly revealing who we are and what we are like. In that sense all of life is a confession. It is up to us as believers to make the supreme confession: that we are

Christ's, that our hearts belong to him and our lives are devoted to him.

Note the urgency, the nature, and the reward of this confession as placed before us by Jesus himself.

Its Urgency

Take a close look at the setting in which these words are found. Note four specific emphases:

First, Jesus addressed himself to the Jews, people who had enjoyed abundant revelation. They had Moses and the prophets; they had been given abundant light, they were highly privileged.

Second, their own claim placed them under obligation. They prided themselves in being the children of Abraham. To them that was equivalent to being children of God.

Third, there was Jesus' own extended ministry in their midst. For three years and more he had proclaimed the gospel to them in the words he spoke and in the miracles he performed.

Fourth, many had not believed, and many more in this world had not even heard the good news of salvation. The need was acute. The proclamation of the gospel must continue. For that reason he had sent out "the seventy;" he had declared that his people are the light of the world. His followers are witnesses, they must go to all the world to share the good news.

Obviously, this tells us that those who have heard the gospel are under tremendous obligation. They are Christ's representatives and wherever they are, wherever they go, and whatever they do, they must acknowledge or confess Christ.

How does this apply to us? As individual believers and as a church we have a sacred duty. We claim to be Christians. Many of us have been baptized in Jesus' name; we have been surrounded by heavenly light and mercy all of our lives; we profess to be Christ's followers, living members of His church. He loved us and purchased us by his shed blood. He is our Savior and Lord. We have declared that we wish to serve him not because of external pressures or legal requirements but because of the inner compulsion of love. A. W. Tozer once said "Duty must become desire." This has happened to us even though our desire is not yet perfect.

How can we be indifferent or blind to the world's great need? All around us are men and women without God or hope in the world. They are dying in sin. We must heed the call, the command of God, to show and tell. Shall we not obey? Shall we not acknowledge Christ? The need is great. Our Lord expects us to be faithful.

He who has said "Come unto me," also says, "Go into all the world and preach the good news to all creation" (Mark 16:15). Without him we can do nothing. We must come to him to receive both pardoning and enabling grace. Only then can we enjoy the blessings of the gospel and demonstrate them to others. The world needs Christians who are committed, believers who reflect the gospel of Christ. We must acknowledge him in all our ways.

Its Nature

What does it mean to acknowledge or confess Christ? Note first of all, that this is a positive requirement. You have likely heard the story about the late President Calvin Coolidge who, after returning from a worship service was asked about the sermon and replied, "The minister preached about sin." When his wife inquired what the minister had said about sin, Coolidge replied, "He was against it."

If in the Bible there are many things which the Bible condemns, then God's children must be against them. There is a negative side to Christianity. But that is by no means the whole of it or even its most prominent feature. Acknowledging Christ is more than protest.

We are challenged by Jesus to be positive. Our lives must reflect dedication, a loyalty to the gospel which is displayed not in a manner which repels but with a winsomeness which attracts and invites attention not to ourselves but to God. Christianity is:

A religion to which we adhere

A truth we confess

A power we experience

A life we live

A message we proclaim.

The central theme of our message is Jesus Christ. As he says, we must confess him. We do so essentially by emphasizing his saving power and his sovereign claim. He is both Jesus the Savior, and Christ the Lord.

Our acknowledgment of Christ must be all-inclusive. We must confess him before men — not only in church where the atmosphere is friendly, but also in the world where we are confronted with denial and opposition. Just read the context in which his admonition is found. You will find a vivid warning of the dangers to be faced and of the persecution to be expected, all introduced by his statement, "I am sending you out like sheep among wolves" (Matt. 10:16). A bit later he adds, "Do not suppose that I have come to bring peace to the earth. I did not come to bring peace, but a sword" (Matt. 10:34).

It is required of us that we manifest who we are and what we do in every relationship and area of life. We cannot do that perfectly, but we must do it consistently. Does not the Bible tell us we must be faithful even unto death?

In a certain sense we appreciate and applaud whole-hearted consecration. When we see missionaries and others sacrificing for the cause of Christ, we lend our support. But remember the command of Christ comes much closer to home than that. It means that those of us who are employers must be Christian employers. It means that employees must perform their tasks as an assignment from God. It means that in our homes and families, husbands and wives, parents and children, brothers and sisters, act like Christians if that is what they confess to be.

Each day should begin with the prayer, "Lord, what would you have me do?" and every day should end with a humble confession of failures but also a thankful recognition of having been used in Christ's service. Blessed are they in whose lives the authority and love of Christ are supreme.

Some years ago I had opportunity to observe a man who established a reputation for his industriousness and honesty. All who had dealings with him, respected him. He lived on a high plane. When I had opportunity to engage him in conversation he gave me a thumbnail sketch of his origin, his background, and of his goal in life. He said: "I was born in Damascus, I was converted in Detroit, I am serving the Lord in Grand Rapids, and I am on the way to the New Jerusalem." What a beautiful confession! He spoke it and he lived it.

Its Reward

Jesus says that if we acknowledge him, he will acknowledge us. That is his promise. When we speak of a reward we understand, of course, that it is not something we earn but something which is given us out of pure grace. Our right to it lies not in our merit, but in God's promise.

What did Jesus mean when he declared that he would

acknowledge us before his Father in heaven? We turn to Scripture for enlightenment. Basically it means three things.

First, he acknowledged his followers at the time of his ascension. At the time they were relatively few in number but he did not return to heaven as a failure. He could point to a loyal band of disciples whom he had brought to faith in him. They were the firstfruits of many who would come from every direction to enter into the kingdom of heaven. Ultimately they would be a countless multitude.

Again, Jesus acknowledges his followers by his constant intercession for them before the throne of God. Knowing their needs and aware of their struggles, he pleads in perfect accord with the Father's will. And on the basis of his perfect sacrifice, his prayer is always answered. We receive showers of blessing.

And finally, Jesus acknowledges his disciples when he returns to judge all men and nations. That will be the time when all things are set straight. Those who have not confessed him shall be at his left hand to hear the pronouncement of doom, but believers shall stand at his right hand to hear his cheering words, "Come, you who are blessed by my Father; take your inheritance, the kingdom prepared for you since the creation of the world" (Matt. 25:34). He acknowledges them as his very own. He has kept them and by grace they have been faithful and true. They are the ones who have acknowledged him.

It is interesting to note how their commitment is described. They lived out their faith, their lives were indeed a confession. Listen to what Jesus says of them:

> For I was hungry and you gave me something to eat, I was thirsty and you gave me something to drink, I was a stranger and you invited me in, I needed clothes and you clothed me, I was sick and you looked after me, I was in prison and you came to visit me (Matt. 25:35–36).

To acknowledge Christ, we need Christ. Coming to him again and again in faith, seeking him in prayer, feeding on his word, and being refreshed and nourished at his table, we are able and eager to serve. We gain new insight into his grace and our hope of glory is revived. In the meantime we continue in faithful service of him, confessing him as our Savior and King.

13

Count Your Blessings

From the fullness of his grace we have all received one blessing after another (John 1:16).

A. **The Source of Our Blessings**
  1. The Word who became flesh
      a) Fullness of deity
      b) Fullness of power
      c) Fullness of grace
  2. Dispels doubt and fear
B. **The Nature of Our Blessings**
  1. We have received
      a) Light from above—we are led to the way
      b) Life everlasting—we are led in the way
  2. Then blessings are
      a) Undeserved—they are ours by grace alone
      b) Abundant—one blessing after another
      c) Experienced—"We have received"—they are ours
C. **Our Response**
  1. Deep humility
  2. Profound gratitude
  3. Hopeful expectancy
  4. Eternal praise

T oday at the table of the Lord we reflect on the goodness of God. Having examined our lives by way of preparation, we are aware of our unworthiness. We realize that it is only by grace that we have both the opportunity and desire to observe this holy sacrament instituted by Christ for the very purpose of giving us assurance that our sins are forgiven.

The goodness of God is greater than we can measure; it exceeds all thought and imagination. The Bible speaks of it in many ways, but nowhere do we see it more clearly than in the cross of Christ. Though our sin is very great, the grace of God is far greater. As Paul said, "But where sin increased, grace increased all the more" (Rom. 5:20).

So we sing:

> Marvelous grace of our loving Lord,
> Grace that exceeds our sin and our guilt,
> Yonder on Calvary's mount outpoured,
> There where the blood of the Lamb was spilt.
>
> Sin and despair like the sea waves cold,
> Threaten the soul with infinite loss;
> Grace that is greater, yes, grace untold,
> Points to the refuge, the mighty cross.
>
> Julia H. Johnston

Experiencing that grace, our soul is flooded with joy. I am reminded of a little boy who was celebrating his birthday. What a special day! His father and mother, brothers and sisters were so nice to him. Everything was wonderful! When at the end of the day mother listened to his evening prayer and tucked him in bed she asked him if he liked the gift he had received. Then she reminded him that all good things come from God. Then the little fellow exclaimed: "God is gooder than we think."

How very true! We learn lessons from children with their simple faith. The psalmist pointed to that long ago when he said, "From the lips of children and infants you have ordained praise" (Ps. 8:2). Yes, God is "gooder" than we think.

To enumerate and assess the blessings of God is impossible of course but the challenge to make the attempt brings a new and deeper sense of our indebtedness to him.

The Source of Our Blessings

The text points us first of all to the source of our blessings. They flow from Christ, the incarnate word. It is out of his fullness that "we have all received one blessing after another."

We interpret that fullness in the light of the beautiful and profound description which precedes:

> In the beginning was the Word,
>   and the Word was with God,
>   and the Word was God. . . .
> Through him all things were made. . . .
> In Him was life, and that life was the light of men. . . .
> The Word became flesh and lived for a while among us
>   . . . full of grace and truth . . . (John 1:1, 3 – 4, 14).

Obviously the "fullness" referred to is the fullness of deity. The Son of God assumed our human nature; he "became flesh and lived among us," but he was and remained God.

It is significant that John should underscore this fact. His Gospel appeared later than those of Matthew, Luke, and Mark, and was written at a time when the deity of Christ was being questioned and even denied; a denial which John vigorously opposes.

As true believers, we would not think of challenging the fact that Jesus was the Son of God, but John's emphasis serves to remind us that we have received heavenly treasures from a heavenly source. Even the bread and wine, which symbolize the broken body and shed blood of Christ, come from the hand and heart of God. In faith we partake of heavenly food and drink.

Who among us can mend broken hearts? Who can heal the malignancy deep within the human spirit? Who can rescue sinners from their misery? Who can impart the hope and joy of eternal life? Only God! These blessings, unique, infinite, and eternal, come from our heavenly Father who has opened for us a never-failing fountain of mercy in his Son, Jesus Christ. We sing, and well we should: "Praise God, from whom all blessings flow."

It follows, as John clearly indicates, that as the incarnate word, the Son of God, manifested "fullness of power." He is the one through whom all things were made. That same majestic omnipotence is revealed in our redemption.

No doubt it has happened to you that when you wanted to buy a certain item, you discovered that it was unavailable. The supply had run out. That never happens when you turn to God with any need or request. Sometimes, for our own good, God answers our petitions in a manner different from what we asked or expected but he is never "caught short." He never says "I'm sorry, I would like to help you but cannot do so just now." Inability is foreign to God.

Fullness of deity! Fullness of power! And to this John adds the thought found in the text itself, "fullness of grace." The Son of God is not only able, he is willing and eager to supply our every need.

Therefore, let faith in Jesus Christ banish your fears and triumph over any vexing doubts that trouble your mind. As you sit at his table, partake of his feast, and look to the cross on which he suffered and died, Be assured of his love and believe that you are blest forever. For this is the sure promise of God, "that neither death nor life, neither angels nor demons, neither the present nor the future, nor any powers, neither height nor death, nor anything else in all creation, will be able to separate us from the love of God that is in Christ Jesus our Lord" (Rom. 8:38–39).

In Jesus we find divine sufficiency. Other people have been used to transmit divine favors, but not apart from Christ or in the same manner and measure. There is but one God and Savior, "Salvation is found in no one else, for there is no other name under heaven given to men by which we must be saved" (Acts 4:12).

We have a divine and mighty Savior. Ask yourself, "Is there anything He cannot do, anything He has not done, anything He will not do?"

The Nature of Our Blessings

Again we take a brief look at the context where John portrays the incarnate word, the source of our blessings in these words, "In him was life, and the life was the light of men." When this is followed by the statement that Jesus came into this world as the one who was "full of grace and truth" we begin to understand how wonderful are the blessings which are ours in him. Truly we have received one blessing after another.

In connection with sin and temptation, we are forced to admit that "one thing leads to another." That is not only unfortunate; it is tragic. But how wonderful when in an altogether different sense we experience that with regard to the grace of God, "one thing leads to another." We receive blessing upon blessing, more than we have any right to expect except that they are all included in the promises of God.

And so by the grace of God we receive light and life. What we lost by sin is restored in far greater measure in salvation. This is the message of God's word, the good news of the gospel.

With prophetic vision it had been proclaimed; "The people walking in darkness have seen a great light; on those living in the land of the shadow of death a light has dawned" (Isa. 9:2).

And Jesus left no doubt that he was the fulfillment of that vision when he declared, "I am the light of the world. Whoever follows me will never walk in darkness, but will have light of life" (John 8:12).

He came to bring light and life. He not only revealed the way out of the darkness of sin but also opened the way. Through his sacrificial life and death he has delivered us from the darkness of sin and death so that we have new life; so that we may enjoy the comfort he himself expressed, "He who believes in me will live, even though he dies; and whoever lives and believes in me will never die" (John 11:25 – 26).

The words of the text, "we have all received one blessing after another" highlights three aspects of the favor of God. They are undeserved, they are abundant, and they are part of our experience.

In some version the phrase "one blessing after another" is translated "blessing upon blessing" or "grace for grace." This is the indication that the goodness of God has many facets and has many hues, like the rainbow in the clouds.

By "grace" is meant that we receive unmerited favors. Actually we have forfeited every claim. When we take inventory of our attitudes and actions we shame-facedly admit that we increase our guilt every day.

How readily we take offense when we feel wronged or are slighted! We find it difficult to overlook or forgive when we ourselves are hurt or harmed. It is easier to preach forgiveness than to practice it.

But now consider what God does. Though he has every

reason to cast us away, to turn his back on us, he comes to us in all the wonder of his seeking and saving love. He rescues us from depths of degradation and lifts us to heights of exaltation. We may not yet have arrived fully, but we are on the way. Just as the bulb blossoms forth in the tulip, so grace is the promise of glory.

"One blessing after another." Is that not intended to impress on our hearts the abundance of God's favors? If each of us at the close of this service were given the opportunity to relate what God has done for us, the story would never end. It would go on, and on, and each narration would be different because God suits his answers to our needs and circumstance.

> He giveth more grace when the burdens grow greater;
> He sendeth more strength when the labors increase.
> To added affliction, he addeth his mercy;
> To multiplied trials, his multiplied peace.
>
> His love has no limit, his grace has no measure,
> His power has no boundary known unto men;
> For out of his infinite riches in Jesus,
> He giveth, and giveth, and giveth, again.
>
> Annie Johnson Flint

Maybe it is best that we summarize and let each develop the details in his own mind. What more meaningful summary than that provided for us in the Apostles' Creed. Here it is: Believing in God the Father, the Son and the Holy Spirit we know and possess:

> The communion of saints
> The forgiveness of sins
> The resurrection of the body
> The life everlasting.

One other aspect of God's mercies is underscored by John. It is expressed in the words, ". . . we have all received." That means we are not spectators, but participants. We need not look with longing eyes wishing that the riches of God's grace were ours. They are!

Our Response

What should be our response? Let me say it in just a few words in the hope those words will inspire all of us to live in a manner pleasing to God. Let us then at this, the Lord's Table, and at the foot of the cross renew our resolve to cultivate:

Deep humility. We who deserved nothing have received everything.

Profound gratitude. We are indebted to God for all that we have and are.

Living hope. The God of yesterday and today, the God of all grace, is the God of tomorrow.

Eternal praise. Let our lives be a doxology to the greatness and goodness of God.

14

A Wonderful Savior, Jesus our Lord!

And we have seen and testify that the Father sent his Son to be the Savior of the world (1 John 4:14).

While we were still sinners, Christ died for us (Rom. 5:8).

Christ loved the church and gave himself for her to make her holy (Eph. 5:25).

The Son of God, who loved me and gave himself for me (Gal. 2:20).

A. The Savior of the World
  1. The world as created
  2. The world as corrupted by man
  3. The world reclaimed
     a) Not all men are saved
     b) Jesus is Savior of the world
B. The Savior of Sinners
  1. God loved sinners
  2. Jesus died for sinful, unworthy men
     a) In their hopeless condition
     b) Rescuing them by his sacrifice
  3. Stated in unparalleled fashion by Paul
C. The Savior of the Church
  1. True believers everywhere
  2. The redeemed, God's possession
  3. Resulting in blessed spiritual fellowship
D. And, our Savior Too
  1. Personal experience of grace
  2. Wonderful assurance

A wonderful Savior is Jesus my Lord." That is the deep conviction and joyous confession of a believer in Christ. He, our Savior, is prominent in our prayers, in our conversations, in our worship together, and in our witness to others. Gathered as we are at the Lord's Table, he is uppermost in our minds.

But though we know him well and love him much, he is actually far greater than we think or imagine. He is all-glorious.

We see the "wonderfulness" of our Savior:

In his identity. He is man but also much more than man. He is the Son of God.

In his mission. The task he performed required divine power and compassion.

In the scope of his saving power. He came, as the above passages clearly indicate, to save the world, to save sinners, to save the church, to save you and me.

The Savior of the World

The world in its original state did not need redemption. In the beginning, as fashioned by the hand of God, it was perfect, a surpassingly beautiful home for all earthly creatures and especially for man created in God's image.

Read the opening words of Scripture which present a picture of this world in its pristine beauty, a world reflecting the splendor of its Creator and intended for his praise. And it was autographed, declaring the glory, wisdom, power, and goodness of its maker.

We never weary of the psalmist's response to the awe inspiring display of divine splendor: "The heavens declare the glory of God; the skies proclaim the work of his hands" (Ps. 19:1).

Perhaps it was that passage and many others in Scripture, accompanied by personal observation, which caused James Herriot to preface his charming books with the simple but profound words:

> All things bright and beautiful,
> All creatures great and small,
> All things wise and wonderful,
> The Lord God made them all.
>   Cecil Francis Alexander

But if we are surrounded with evidences of God's greatness, why do we also see so much that is sordid and ugly? There is a reason and that reason is not to be found in God but in man who challenged God's authority and transgressed the divine command. That is the horrendous happening, the tragic event—man fell into sin, dragging the whole world with him into degradation and misery.

In Genesis 3 we read that God, in pronouncing judgment, said to Adam, "Cursed is the ground because of you," and in chapter 6 we read "Now the earth was corrupt in God's sight and was full of violence." And centuries later Paul refers to this present evil world as "groaning as in the pains of childbirth right up to the present time" (Rom. 8:22).

And the notion that the world was gradually getting better, or could be salvaged by education or human ingenuity, has been exposed as utter folly. By nature men are wicked; they will not turn to God and as a result this world is a world of poverty and persecution, war and bloodshed, crime and violence, danger and death. Would you agree with the late Dr. Samuel Zwemer, veteran missionary well acquainted with conditions in this twentieth-century world, that this world was "never so large; never so small; and never so needy"?

The situation is desperate. Must we conclude that the damage is beyond repair? Is there no possibility of reclamation? Is there no hope?

That would be true were it not for the boundless power and mercy of God. He alone could save and the fact is that he did, he does, and he will. Listen to the message of positive and blessed assurance given in his Word:

"God was reconciling the world to himself in Christ" (2 Cor. 5:19).

". . . the Father has sent his Son to be the Savior of the world" (1 John 4:14).

God refused to capitulate. He refused to relinquish title to the world he had made. Satan and sinful men could not possibly succeed in their attempt to take control. The great creator, the gracious provider, becomes the blessed redeemer. Through his Son, Jesus Christ, he rescues the world and reconciles it to himself.

This does not mean that all men are saved. The requirement of penitence for sin and faith in the Savior is proclaimed and maintained. But in a very important sense Jesus is the Savior of the world.

First, through a worldwide publication of the gospel members of all tribes and nations hear the good news of divine redemption and experience its saving power. Secondly, the world as "cosmos," the handiwork and cherished possession of God, shall not be allowed to pass into oblivion or be totally destroyed. At the end of time, in keeping with God's promise, we shall see and enjoy "a new heaven and a new earth, the home of righteousness" (2 Peter 3:13). Our Savior, whose redeeming work and sacrifice we commemorate, is a Savior wonderful indeed. He is the Savior of the world. He has done what no one else could do.

The Savior of Sinners

The Bible demands that, loving God first and most, we must love our neighbor as we love ourselves. And Jesus gave that command a new dimension when he instructed us to love our enemies. We ask: Is that fair; is that reasonable? Who of us can live up to that injunction?

If that is your feeling, think of what God did. Paul tells us in Romans 5 ". . . while we were yet sinners Christ died for us." God certainly had more reason to be unforgiving than we have. Yet he sacrificed his Son to save those who were his enemies.

The impact of Paul's statement is even greater when we read it in context:

Very rarely will anyone die for a righteous man, though for a good man someone might possibly dare to die. But God demonstrates his own love to us in this: While we were still sinners, Christ died for us (Rom. 5:7 – 8).

Life is precious. It is true enough that we hesitate to sacrifice it for deserving people or for a worthy cause. We are human. But Christ reveals the love that is divine. And if that were not so, you and I would not be saved for all of us are guilty of disobedience and transgression.

But why should God do what he did; why did he send his Son to save those who did not deserve such love and could not expect it? The only reason is this: God is love and in his infinite love he took compassion on poor, lost sinners who could never be saved or find their way back without his intervention.

Every day we hear of instances where people witness serious trouble or are aware of critical need but refuse to become involved because of disinterest, fear, or the pursuit of their own interests. Like the priest and Levite in the parable of the good Samaritan they look away or pass by on the other side. Ask yourself: Do I care enough?

Shall we then say that God is different or unique? That would be a false comparison. God is not merely different or unique, he is God. His love is infinite, beyond all comprehension.

In his book, *Beneath the Cross of Jesus,* the gifted author, R. E. O. White has given us an eloquent, and to me an unforgettable, portrayal of what God did:

> Of course there is truth behind the notion that God sits enthroned above the flood, beyond the reach of the storms and conflicts and changes that vex our lives. It is a relief to look away from the decay and uncertainty of life to God above the struggle, the unshaken Rock beneath which we find shelter, the unmistakable Refuge to which we flee, the untroubled Anchorage of our restless hearts. But beside the truth of God's transcendence—God the Supreme, the "Wholly Other" the Bible sets a second truth: that God stepped down amid the storm and pain and mire and sin, to bear our griefs and carry our sorrows—because He cared. The whole difference between ourselves and Him in this respect lies here: that we are in the conflict and the shame largely because we deserve to be, wholly because we cannot help it; He is in it because He *chose* to be. He was immune: He chose for love's sake to become entangled. We see God upon the cross.

The thought expressed must surely have been set in motion by the classic statement, emphasizing not only the Father's love but also his Son's willing and complete sacrifice, found in Philippians 2:6–8.

> Who being in very nature God,
>   did not consider equality with God
>   something to be grasped,

> but made himself nothing,
>   taking the very nature of a servant,
>   being made in human likeness.
> And being found in appearance as a man,
>   he humbled himself
>   and became obedient to death —
>   even death on a cross.

Yes, Jesus is the Savior of sinners. He who welcomed publicans and sinners, and ministered to their needs; he, who as the Good Shepherd, sought and found his wandering sheep; he came from his heavenly home to a sinful world to die on the cross — the cross of Calvary, that by his sacrifice men might be saved. How shameful, yet how fitting that he should be nailed to Calvary's cross between two sinners, there to demonstrate his saving power and grace! Is that the gracious invitation and promise you hear in the Word? Come to the holy sacrament of the Lord's Supper in accordance with that comforting encouragement: "Only believe!"

The Savior of the Church

The church is more than a building where we worship, more than a congregation of which we are members, more than a denomination to which we belong. It is all true believers; all the people of God.

Active in the congregation and loyal to the denomination which we love, let us clearly see and appreciate the Church of God in the truly biblical sense: people called out of darkness, dedicated to Christ, and though assembled in many different groups and congregations, one in the Lord; one in their faith, hope, and love.

God never intended that the song of redemption would be a solo; he planned it as a grand oratorio, a glorious and resounding symphony of praise. So he saves sinners one by one, he certainly does not ignore families as channels of his mercy; but remember that through it all he redeems a church.

When we hear the church criticized and derided, and we are disappointed because of her faults and failings, let us call to mind what the Bible says, "Christ loved the church and gave himself up for her to make her holy" (Eph. 5:25).

The church is God's precious possession, it is his vineyard, his temple, the body of Christ, the bride of Christ. What a price he paid for her redemption! How you and I should love "the church of God, which he bought with his own blood" (Acts 20:28).

There is no more blessed communion than our fellowship with God. Through Christ by grace he is our Father in heaven. And when, as God's people, forgiven and cleansed in the blood of Calvary's cross, we gather at the Lord's Table we experience a togetherness with God and one another which is a foretaste of heaven's perfect bliss.

Let us put aside those things which hinder and interfere and let us express our obedience to the new commandment Christ gave us, that we love one another even as Christ himself loved us. Then heaven will be in our hearts and our hearts will be in heaven. And with deeper sincerity and feeling we sing:

> Blest be the tie that binds
> Our hearts in Christian love,
> The fellowship of kindred minds
> Is like to that above.
>   John Fawcett, 1782

And, our Savior Too

Does it ever occur to you that maybe as far as God is concerned you "are lost in the crowd." With the whole universe to uphold and govern, with numberless creatures dependent on his care, with millions and millions of men in dire need, and with his widespread church turning to him in constant and varied supplication, how can he be mindful of you and me? Does he even notice whether we are present or absent at his table?

When we think in that fashion, we speak in terms of our own limitations and by human standards.

We need to remember that God watches the birds of the air and clothes the lilies of the field. Nothing escapes his attention and no one is too insignificant for his concern. Jesus could say to us as he said to his disciples more than once, "O you of little faith."

Did Jesus not notice Bartimaeus who cried out for mercy? Did he not stop a funeral procession to raise a widow's son? Did he not turn to weeping women who sorrowfully followed him on the way to the cross? And was he not aware of Zaccheus hid among the branches of a sycamore tree?

All doubt of divine interest and concern should be dispelled when we recall Jesus' specific reference to the fact that he knows each one of his sheep by name. There is no chance in the world that when we draw near to him we shall be overlooked or ignored. He who has saved, keeps and sanctifies us until we are perfectly holy and our salvation is complete.

If sinners are not turned away, shall not saints of God, no matter how weak or small, be welcomed with open arms. Without a doubt! "He who did not spare his own Son, but gave him up for us all—how will he not also, along with him, graciously give us all things" (Rom. 8:32).

At the cross, grace for sinners and saints, grace for you and me.

> Grace, grace, God's grace
> Grace that will pardon and cleanse within
> Grace, grace, God's grace
> Grace that is greater than all our sin.
>   Julia H. Johnston

15

Behold, the Lamb of God!

Look, the Lamb of God, who takes away the sin of the world (John 1:29).

A. Abraham's Sacrifice of his Son
 1. Required by God
 2. Accomplished in spirit
 3. Awaiting God's provision
B. The Passover
 1. The blood shed for atonement
 2. The feast provided for strength
C. Further Revelation
 1. Psalm 22 prefigures the cross
 2. Isaiah 53 describes the cross
 3. I Corinthians 5:7 interprets the cross
D. God and Men at Calvary
E. Revelation Supplies Divine Comfort
 1. In the Lamb desperately needed
 2. In the Lamb appointed by God
 3. In the Lamb able to serve, worthy to open the book of life
 4. In the Lamb triumphantly acclaimed

Shall we walk through the garden of God's word exploring the beauty and fragrance of its truths? If you have done so frequently, even regularly, you know better than many other Christians that there is still much to learn. Focus your attention on what the Bible has to say about "the Lamb of God."

The sacrament we are about to observe, the Lord's Supper, directs us to that Lamb, the sacrificial Lamb, who suffered and died for our sins on the altar of Calvary's cross.

Abraham's Sacrifice of his Son

We begin with the story of Abraham as he faces the supreme test of his faith. God says to him "Take your son, your only son Isaac, whom you love, and go to the region of Moriah. Sacrifice him there as a burnt offering on one of the mountains I will tell you about" (Gen. 22:2).

Can you imagine the turmoil in Abraham's soul? These are the questions with which he battles: Why would God demand a human sacrifice? Why must he sacrifice his son, his only son? Why must he sacrifice Isaac whose promised birth had been Abraham's sustaining hope for many years?

Why does God confuse him? For God has said ". . . it is through Isaac that your offspring will be reckoned" (Gen. 21:12), referring very clearly to that throng of descendants which shall be in number as the stars of heaven and as the sand on the seashore. According to that assurance Isaac must live. Now God says he must die. Does God contradict himself; is he unfaithful to his word?

And why must Abraham make a three-day journey to Mount Moriah with such a heavy burden on his heart? Why not finish it now?

Abraham meets the test. He does what God commands. The fact that at the last moment Isaac was spared does not detract from Abraham's obedience. His intention and willingness was enough. God took the will for the deed. This is evident from the divine evaluation and approbation expressed in the Book of Hebrews: "By faith Abraham, when God tested him, offered Isaac as a sacrifice. Abraham reasoned that God could raise the dead, and figuratively speaking, he did receive Isaac back from death" (Heb. 11:17, 19).

What stupendous faith. Abraham believed in something that had never happened. He refused to underestimate God and trusted that with God all things are possible.

When Isaac said, " 'Father . . . The fire and the wood are here, . . . but where is the lamb for the burnt offering?' Abraham answered, 'God himself will provide the lamb . . .' " (Gen. 22:7 – 8). Isaac was spared by a voice from heaven which stopped the descent of the upraised knife, "Abraham looked up and there in a thicket he saw a ram caught by its horns. He went over and took the ram and sacrificed it as a burnt offering instead of his son" (Gen. 22:13).

Divine provision as Abraham expected! A substitution to be sure—but one totally symbolic and not sufficient as an offering for sin.

Though Jesus later said of him, "Your father Abraham rejoiced at the thought of seeing my day; he saw it and was glad," (John 8:56), that patriarch who exhibited such magnificent faith and was blessed with unusual insight (or foresight) could not have envisioned the glorious fulfillment of his believing expectancy.

As New Testament believers we know the story, the sequel to Abraham's statement, "God himself will provide the lamb. . . ." He has done so. "Look, the Lamb of God!" The Son of God offering himself and sacrificed by God the Father in atonement for our sins. How great is the goodness and grace of God. Take refuge in the cross and find forgiveness, eternal security, and peace in the love of God.

The Passover

We move on to the description of the first Passover instituted by God at the time of Israel's departure from Egypt.

Through Moses, God instructs his people that they shall take a lamb, one for each family; they "are to take some of the blood and put it on the sides and tops of the door-frames of the houses where they eat the lambs. Eat it in haste; it is the Lord's Passover" (Exod. 12:7, 11).

The symbolism is clear. Atonement is necessary to be delivered from the judgment of God, and strength is required for the arduous journey to the promised land.

Annually Israel must observe this sacrament, a reminder of past deliverance from the bondage of Egypt and prophetic of that greater deliverance still to come—salvation from sin.

Further Revelation

This is the story of man's sin and God's grace. Sin must be punished with a penalty too great for any man to bear. But in his great mercy the Lord will provide. Consider that astounding provision as further unfolded for us in Scripture:

First the prefiguration of the cross found in Psalm 22:

. . . they have pierced my hands and feet
They divide my garments among them and cast lots for
    my clothing.

Next the prophetic description given in Isaiah 53:

But he was pierced for our transgressions,
    he was crushed for our iniquities. . . .
He was oppressed and afflicted,
    Yet he did not open his mouth;
he was led like a lamb to the slaughter,
    and as a sheep before her shearers is silent,
    so he did not open his mouth.

And then look the commentary by the apostle Paul, so cryptic yet freighted with meaning, "For Chirst, our Passover Lamb, has been sacrificed" (1 Cor. 5:7).

You know what is meant. God himself has provided the
unblemished lamb; the Son of God is the Lamb of God.
The Gospels provide the account of his death on the cross
of Calvary where human sin in all its ugliness and crimi-
nality is unmasked, and divine grace is climactically revealed.

God and Men at Calvary

Listen once again to the story of God's redeeming love:
"Two other men, both criminals, were also led out with him
to be executed. When they came to the place called The
Skull, there they crucified him along with the criminals —
one on his right, the other on his left. Jesus said, 'Father,
forgive them, for they do not know what they are doing' "
(Luke 23:32 – 34).

If they did not know, God knew. While they were com-
mitting the most ghastly crime of history, God was paying
the price of his people's redemption by the death of his Son.

Was it effective? It had to be and it was. Thankfully we
accept and cherish the sequel in the immediately succeeding
paragraph:

> One of the criminals who hung there hurled insults at him:
> "Aren't you the Christ? Save yourself and us!" But the
> other criminal rebuked him. "Don't you fear God," he
> said, "since you are under the same sentence? We are pun-
> ished justly, for we are getting what our deeds deserve. But
> this man has done nothing wrong." Then he said, "Jesus,
> remember me when you come into your kingdom." Jesus
> answered him, "I tell you the truth, today you will be with
> me in paradise" (Luke 23:39 – 43).

Now once for all the sacrifice has been brought. Promises
are fulfilled, punishment and penalty are removed. God has
bought and wrought salvation. "Look, the Lamb of God!"

Are you washed in the blood of the Lamb? If you in faith celebrate the Supper of the Lord, the broken bread is a sign and seal that all your sins are forgiven, that you are a child of God saved by grace.

One more aspect of the cross demands your attention. If it was for your salvation, never forget that it was intended to glorify God and to magnify Christ, your Savior.

Revelation Supplies Divine Comfort

We turn to the last book of the Bible, the Book of Revelation written by the apostle John while he was in exile on the Isle of Patmos for the sake of the gospel. Can you understand that in his loneliness and bewilderment he is filled with concern for himself and even more for the church?

He is told the terrible things that are going to happen as the church is assailed in every manner and from every direction. At the same time he receives heavenly visions full of cheer and consolation. The heart of the message is this: The crucified Savior is now the living Lord. Those who focus their faith on him need not be afraid. Jesus has gained the victory for himself and the church. He, the Lord of all, is in control and he will direct all that happens for the benefit of his own. They need not be afraid; they are destined to share in his glory.

We are provided an overwhelmingly beautiful background for the life and death of Christ on earth. Once again we are called and permitted to behold the Lamb of God—but now from the perspective of God's sovereign will and plan.

In Revelation 5 John shares with us his vision of "The Scroll and the Lamb." When it was evident that no one was able to open the scroll to carry out God's redemptive program, John tells us that he "wept and wept." He was overcome by the hopelessness of the situation. But suddenly he hears a voice commanding him, "Do not weep! See, the

Lion of the tribe of Judah, the Root of David has triumphed. He is able to open the scroll and its seven seals" (Rev. 5:5). We are taught the necessity of the cross.

And amazingly that Lion of the tribe of Judah is a Lamb sent out into all the earth. He takes "the scroll from the right hand of him who sat on the throne" and the elders and the living creatures sing a new song:

> You are worthy to take the scroll
>   and to open its seals,
> because you were slain,
>   and with your blood purchased men for God
>   from every tribe and language and people and nation.
> You have made them to be a kingdom and priests to
>   serve our God,
>   and they will reign on the earth (Rev. 5:9–10).

What a vivid picture of the meaning of the cross and of the crucified Christ. A picture which is indelibly printed on our minds by the emphatic reference to "the book of life belonging to the Lamb that was slain from the creation of the world!" (Rev. 13:8). Perish the thought that the cross of Christ was an accident, an unavoidable tragedy. It was the very essence of God's redemptive plan. It had to happen—and it did. Praise to his glorious name!

It is for us who have been saved by the blood of Christ to join the elders and living creatures around the throne, along with thousands and thousands of angels in the excellent song:

> Worthy is the Lamb, who was slain,
>   to receive power and wealth and wisdom and
>   strength
>   and honor and glory and praise! . . .
> To him who sits on the throne and to the Lamb
>   be praise and honor and glory and power
>   for ever and ever. Amen.
>   (Rev. 5:12–13)

A song for holy angels and a song for men redeemed from sin. Is it natural to be saddened by the cross? Of course, it was our sins that nailed him to the tree.

And yet we glory in the cross. It gives reason for joy. It is the cross of our salvation. It is so fitting that our solemn commentary of our Savior's death should at the same time be a thankful and happy celebration. We see his humiliation in the light of his exaltation.

Behold the Lamb of God! Indeed:

The Lord has provided.

Christ sacrificed himself on the cross.

Sinners have been saved.

Angels sing his praise.

The saints of God rejoice.

O Lamb of God, still keep me near to thy wounded side!
'Tis only there is safety and peace I can abide.
What foes and snares surround me! What doubts and
    fears within!
The grace that sought and found me, alone can keep me
    clean.
'Tis only in thee hiding, I know my life secure;
Only in thee abiding, the conflict can endure.
Thine arm the victory gaineth o'er every hateful foe;
Thy love my heart sustaineth in all its care and woe.
                                          James G. Deck, 1842

16

Living in
Remembrance of Him

*But you, dear friends, build yourselves up in your most
holy faith and pray in the Holy Spirit. Keep yourselves in
God's love as you wait for the mercy of our Lord Jesus
Christ to bring you to eternal life* (Jude 20, 21).

A. **Build**
    1. The twofold implication
        a) That we are believers
        b) That the faith is the foundation
    2. Remember
        a) The danger of self-deception
        b) We must be built up in the faith
        c) We must know and obey the Word
B. **Pray**
    1. Prayer as supreme fellowship
    2. Prayer is
        a) The avenue to God's favor
        b) Response to divine invitation
        c) Exercise of a glorious privilege
        d) Language of the believing soul
        e) Upreach of the needy heart
    3. Pray "in the Holy Spirit"
        a) Prompted by the Spirit
        b) Directed and controlled by the Spirit
C. **Keep**
    1. Exercising the faith he has given
    2. Using the means he has provided

D. Wait
   1. We expect
   2. We prepare
   3. We persevere

We are not our own; we belong to God. The redeemed life he gave us must be dedicated to his praise. Because it is our desire to live for him we use the means of grace he has provided, and when we do so our desire is intensified. How then shall we give expression to the supreme goal of our salvation?

Jude, a brother of Jesus who in self-effacing manner introduces himself as "A servant of Jesus Christ" provides for us a summary of what we should do in order to realize life's exalted purpose and to enjoy ourselves in the service of God. He tells us we must: *Build, Pray, Keep,* and *Wait.*

Build

Jude calls us to, ". . . build yourselves up in your most holy faith." The implication is twofold. We are in the faith and our faith is the foundation on which we can and should build.

Is it true that you are in the faith; that you are a true believer in Jesus Christ as your Savior and Lord? Is your confession of him sincere?

That question must not be easily dismissed. To be a Christian involves more than membership in the church and involvement in religious exercise. Jesus warns that some who consider themselves followers of Christ and who expect to enter into glory when he returns deceive themselves only to be disillusioned when it is too late. They will have cried "Lord, Lord!" and will point to works presumably done for him, but they will be disowned. Their godliness is only an outward appearance, not a genuine commitment.

For that reason — the danger of self-deception — the apostle Paul admonishes members of the church, "Examine yourselves to see whether you are in the faith; test yourselves" (2 Cor. 13:5). And it is in connection with the Lord's Supper that he issues an urgent call accompanied by a stern warning: "A man ought to examine himself before he eats of the bread and drinks of the cup. For anyone who eats and drinks without recognizing the body of the Lord eats and drinks judgment on himself" (1 Cor. 11:28, 29).

The genuineness of our faith must be expressed in our lives. That confession is not momentary or spasmodic; it embraces all that we do or say.

We are required to build ourselves up in the most holy faith. The foundation of our lives is not some ancient philosophy or modern ideology, it is not prevalent thought or popular opinion, it is not our own notions or ideas. Rather, it is the will of God, revealed in his Word; taught, exemplified, and fulfilled in Jesus Christ; given to the apostles, and transmitted to the church for continuous practice and proclamation. On this all believers must build. Their lives must be an expression of God's truth.

To accomplish this, it is imperative that we seek intimate fellowship with God through the study of his word. To build on the faith we must be built up in the faith. Consecration in a corrupt and sinful world involves growing knowledge of the divinely inspired Scriptures. God's word must control our thought and action. It provides an unerring guide for the journey of life.

By neglecting the study of Scripture we hamper our spiritual development, we fail to reach our potential, and to that extent we fall short of that wholehearted service which brings joy to our own hearts, truly benefits others, and honors God's name. According to the Gospels, Jude and his brothers at first did not believe in Jesus (John 7:5), but by the time of Christ's resurrection and ascension they had found their place in the circle of believers for, as indicated in Acts 1:14, they were among those who gathered in an upper room at Jerusalem "joined together constantly in prayer."

Is the Bible unerring, dependable? Steeping ourselves in the knowledge of the gospel we develop an ever-clearer understanding of God's will and growing assurance that we are walking in God's way which is the way of sanctification. Obedience to God is the avenue of blessing, joy, and peace. God's word is holy and promotes holiness within and without, separation from evil and consecration to God.

We must exercise our faith by building ourselves up in the faith! A clear and unmistakable expression of it in our outward conduct is not possible without personal and united perusal and appropriation of the gospel. Like a tree: to grow up, we must grow down.

May our observance of the Lord's Supper be an indication that the word of God is precious to us and may it motivate us to return to that word with even greater eagerness.

Pray

Jude continues his instruction with, ". . . pray in the Holy Spirit."

Of course, prayer is the supreme fellowship which we can enjoy on earth. It is communion with God, vitally necessary for enjoyment of his blessings and for involvement in the program of his kingdom. Without prayer a man can neither receive or give.

The Bible describes prayer in many ways. We are taught that prayer is: coming to God, opening one's mouth, asking, seeking, desiring, calling, crying, beseeching, sighing, pouring out one's heart, appearing before God's face, bowing, kneeling, lifting up hands, thanking, praising, worshiping.

May I suggest a summary as food for thought. Prayer is:

The avenue to God's favor.

Response to divine invitation.

Exercise of glorious privilege.

Language of the believing soul.

Upreach of the needy heart.

Gilbert Thomas has emphasized the last element, "upreach of the needy heart," in a beautiful fashion:

> There is a bridge, whereof the span
> Is rooted in the heart of man,
> And reaches, without pile or rod,
> Unto the Great White Throne of God.
> Its traffic is in human sighs
> Fervently wafted to the skies;
> 'Tis the one pathway from despair:
> And it is called the Bridge of Prayer.

I have no doubt that God's children pray. But prayer is real only when it is sincere. Otherwise it is no more than an inherited bit of propriety, a custom we dare not omit or discard. We must indeed "pray in the Holy Spirit."

That means our communion with God must be prompted by the Spirit, directed, controlled, and sanctified by him. Then our prayers are cleansed from selfishness, victorious over thoughtlessness, and characterized by humble sincerity. Influenced by the Spirit we acknowledge our complete dependence, express genuine love and faith, and seek divine forgiveness and approval. Prayer is the root of the Christian life; we need it to receive grace and to bear fruit.

God speaks to us and we may speak to God. How wonderful that in the quietness at the communion table we may engage in reverent, sincere and holy conversation with God! And we shall know that God who is far above us is in our very midst.

The close relationship between "building yourself in the most holy faith" and the study of God's word is beautifully expressed in a favorite hymn:

> Take time to be holy, speak oft with thy Lord;
> Abide in him always, and feed on His Word. . . .
>
> Take time to be holy, the world rushes on;
> Spend much time in secret with Jesus alone. . . .
>
> Thus led by his Spirit to fountains of love,
> Thou soon shalt be fitted for service above.
> William D. Longstaff

Keep

We know that once we belong to God we are his forever. Once saved, we are always saved. The Bible clearly teaches preservation of the saints. In Psalm 84 it is said, "They go from strength to strength till each appears before God in Zion (Ps. 84:7).

And Jesus stated it in most emphatic fashion when he declared, "And this is the will of him who sent me, that I shall lose none of all that he has given me, but raise them up at the last day" (John 6:39).

Surely, God keeps his own children and those for whom Christ died shall never slip from his grasp. They cannot be lost. He will not allow it.

But that does not mean that we can take our eternal salvation for granted or that we have no responsibility. We must persevere; we must endure to the end. And, as Jude here states, "we must keep ourselves in the love of God."

Using the means God has provided, we must allow nothing to break or interfere with the relationship between ourselves and our heavenly Father. He has expressed his favor in a multitude of ways; he has enveloped us in his love and has bound us to himself through the blood and Spirit of Jesus Christ. Abiding in his love, we shall be filled with strength, confidence, and hope. And ever gazing at the cross we shall sing of his grace:

> O love of God, how strong and true!
> Eternal, and yet ever new,
> Uncomprehended and unbought,
> Beyond all knowledge and all thought.
>
> We read thee best in him who came
> To bear for us the cross of shame;
> Sent by the Father from on high,
> Our life to live, our death to die.
>
> O love of God, our shield and stay
> Through all the perils of our way;
> Eternal love, in thee we rest,
> Forever safe, forever blest.
>
> Horatius Bonar, 1861

Wait

Though we build ourselves up in the faith, pray in the Holy Spirit, and keep ourselves in God's love, on earth and in this life we never attain perfection or reach the fullness of his glory promised us in Scripture. The best is yet to come. We are destined for eternal life in our eternal home.

Scripture teaches that believers have eternal life here and now. They are new creatures and the life which is theirs in Christ shall never die or fade away. But sinlessness, complete holiness and happiness still await. We consider the joy and peace and blessing which is ours and know that we shall have all this and heaven too.

The fact is that those who believe in Christ have been saved, they are being saved, and they shall be saved. They have been reconciled, they are being sanctified, and they shall be glorified.

Saved by Jesus and living in fellowship with him, we look forward to the time of his return. We are eager to see him face to face in all the brightness of his glory, as the Son of God and the Son of man.

Repeatedly the Bible points us to the return of Christ. Its certainty is assured, and its glorious manner is certified and, to some extent, described. It shall be with the sound of a trumpet, accompanied by angels, and on the clouds of heaven. While his enemies shall cringe in fear, his people will break forth in joyous acclaim. It is the day of the Lord, the day when his victory and exaltation is revealed. And it is also the day of our complete redemption. No more sin, no more sorrow, no more death, no more tears. We live in expectation of that "grand finale" for Christ's sake and our own. He shall be glorified and we shall be glorified with him.

Jesus promised that one day, together with him, we would enjoy the great heavenly feast of which the Lord's Supper is a foretaste and preview. Paul instructed the church to commemorate the Lord's Supper "till he comes" that is, until Jesus' blessed return.

Jude reminds us to "wait for the mercy of our Lord Jesus Christ to bring us to eternal life." Jesus will complete the work he has begun and we shall receive a blessed reward, the reward of eternal life not because we have merited it, but because in his mercy he fulfills the promise he has given. He brings about the realization of our hopes and prayers, and will do so in a manner far beyond our expectation.

Persevere in faith, persevere in prayer, persevere in love, persevere in hope. Amid all distractions, discouragements, and disappointment, look to the Savior who came to earth that he might bring us to heaven and know assuredly that he is coming again.

17

Grace Beyond Measure

And my God will meet all your needs according to his glorious riches in Christ Jesus (Phil. 4:19).

A. Personal Confession
   1. Who was Paul?
      a) Theologian, missionary, pastor
      b) A humble child of God
   2. How did he know God?
      a) By training
      b) By conversion
      c) By experience
      d) By revelation
B. Blessed Assurance
   1. Pertains to the future
   2. The future is our worry
   3. The Lord will bless
C. Comprehensive Promise
   1. Not all our desires and wishes
   2. All our needs
      a) In his power — he is able
      b) In his mercy — he is eager
D. Divine Sufficiency
   1. Riches of glory are riches of grace
   2. Abundant provision
      a) Not out of his riches
      b) According to his riches

By divine call and direction the apostle Paul had a prominent part in the birth and development of the congregation at Philippi. For that reason and because of favorable reports of her spiritual vitality this small but growing group of believers has a special place in his heart.

The letter he writes to the Philippians is warm and encouraging, filled with commendation and loving admonition. For us it contains many nuggets of truth which we treasure as a constant source of instruction and inspiration. Here are a few samples:

> ... being confident of this, that he who began a good work in you will carry it on to completion until the day of Christ Jesus (1:6). For to me, to live is Christ and to die is gain (1:21). Rejoice in the Lord always. I will say it again: Rejoice! (4:4). Do not be anxious about anything, but in everything, by prayer and petition, with thanksgiving, present your requests to God. And the peace of God, which transcends all understanding, will guard your hearts and your minds in Christ Jesus (4:6, 7).

Other passages are omitted only because we continue our climb to the superlative thought reserved for the very close of this epistle: "And my God will meet all your needs according to his glorious riches in Christ Jesus." Those words are freighted with meaning. In them personal confession is found.

Personal Confession

The man who says "My God" so simply and sincerely is known to us as the great missionary and theologian of the early New Testament church. He was also a faithful and warm-hearted pastor. When that has been said, we hasten to add that he was a humble child of God. The gospel he proclaimed was a gospel he himself believed. Used of God, he brought others to Christ by whom he himself had been

found. He was first called to faith in Christ and then to the
service of Christ.

He does not hesitate to declare that God is his God. His
testimony is wonderfully jubilant, yet sufficiently subdued
so that it does not obscure what God has done but articu-
lates and reflects that marvelous grace of God. Paul takes
no credit and seeks no praise. He does not parade his spirituality; he can only say, "But by the grace of God I am
what I am . . ." (1 Cor. 15:10).

How did Paul know God? How had that been brought
about? How had Paul learned to know God when all around
him he saw people walking in sin and ignorance? The answer to those questions is varied.

Paul had learned to know God by training and tradition.
Or, to express it differently, he had learned to know God
in covenantal fashion. He was a member of the Hebrew
nation, God's chosen people, and had been raised in a Jew-
ish family. He had received special training in the law and
the prophets, he was thoroughly conversant with Old Testament revelation. He had learned to love "the faith of the
fathers."

That tells us something important. Let those who have
been born or raised in a Christian family never underestimate or despise that privilege. If from infancy you were
so surrounded by spiritual influences that you cannot remember which was the first Bible story you heard or the
first prayer you learned, thank God for the blessing of such
a rich heritage.

But that is not enough. We are not saved by the faith of
godly parents or grandparents. We ourselves must believe.
Our relationship to God must be personal and sincere.
Without that we may have the appearance of godliness
without knowing God.

We see then that Paul knew God by conversion. He had
been turned from sin to God. That is true of all who become

true Christians. That may happen as a crisis, it may involve prolonged struggle, or, as in many instances, it may come by way of gradual development. But let it be definitely understood that conversion is indispensable to a right relationship with God.

Again, Paul knew God by experience. Paul speaks of that in the context where, in connection with varying providential circumstances in his life, he says: "I have learned. . . ."

It is natural for a child to develop. If a child does not grow, something is very wrong. How pathetic if we do not know the Lord better, love him more, and serve him more diligently, than we did a year or several years ago! Does not the Bible declare that we must "grow in the grace and knowledge of our Lord and Savior Jesus Christ" (2 Peter 3:18)?

Consider what it means to know God by training, conversion, and experience. Add it all up and you will arrive at the conclusion that we have learned to know God by revelation. God is not a discovery; he is first of all a disclosure. He has said: "Here I am." He has done that in his Word and through the preaching of that Word. He has made his presence known in the sacraments as well. He meets us and we meet him in blessed communion at the Lord's table.

Blessed Assurance

Life, as you are well aware, has various dimensions. We look back, we look around, we look ahead. Past, present, and future; is that the whole of life?

Not for believers. Their life is characterized by an upward look. For them God is present in every dimension and in every experience. Looking back, they are prompted to acknowledge their sins and also their indebtedness to God for countless blessings. Looking around, they see many reasons for concern. They face moral dangers on every hand and are not qualified in themselves to cope with threats and temptations. And looking ahead, they are apprehensive. The future is unknown and, to a large extent, beyond their control. We, being in the world, are challenged by fear.

But Christians must never despair, they may face the future with confidence. That is Paul's assurance and it should be ours. Why be afraid when we know God is watching over us? Faith dispels fear. The God of yesterday and today is also the God of tomorrow.

I remember an incident which occurred at a conference center. The daily morning Bible Study was preceded by an hour of fellowship — a cup of coffee, a roll, a doughnut, or a cookie, and lots of conversation and laughter. One morning on the way to the assembly hall I saw an old man struggling along the uneven pathway with the help of a cane.

The question was: Should I pass him by with a cheerful "good morning," or should I slow my pace to match his and perhaps embarrass him. I did greet him and then said "It's rather rough going, isn't it?" He said, "Yes," and after a moment's pause he looked at me with a beaming face and added: "But the Lord leads the way." What a preparation for the discussion of Scripture which I was about to lead! And what blessed assurance for us on the road of life!

How it strengthens us to be reminded that God will supply all our needs! We are not left to our own resources or limited to our own strength. We go with God who keeps us under his loving care. He is able and eager to help us in every situation.

In connection with divine providence, Jesus in the Sermon on the Mount pointed to God's care for his creatures, reproached his disciples for their "little faith," and left with them and us the comforting admonition that we should not worry about tomorrow, for our heavenly Father knows our needs and will supply them.

Paul echoes that sentiment. God provided for him and

was doing so even while he was in prison. And that is the truth he would impress on the minds of his fellow believers at Philippi. Trusting in God, they must learn to trust him more and, doing so, they will never be disappointed.

All of us are in need of encouragement. The road of life is not always smooth and God's children are not immune to difficulty and danger. Sometimes we struggle; we are not sure that we can continue to endure. The load becomes awfully heavy and the future seems very dark. We find our help and hope in God.

Comprehensive Promise

In no way does the text assert that God will fulfill all our wants and wishes. That might seem nice, but it would not be good. We don't do that with our children or grand-children. We understand their need of provision, guidance, instruction; their interests are ours. Immature as they are, they need control and even discipline. What they want or desire is not always for their good.

So our heavenly Father decides what is best for us and we should be grateful that he does. We should be happy to let him decide so that all our desires and petitions breath the spirit: "Thy will be done."

In the previous verses Paul emphasizes that he has experienced both hardship and happiness, poverty and plenty. Through it all he has learned the lesson of contentment. He has inner peace. He has been convinced that God's way is the best way.

The congregation at Philippi had expressed its deep affection for Paul by sending him a gift. It had arrived at an opportune time and was gratefully welcomed and received, especially because it was a fruit of faith. What they did, they did in Jesus' name.

But in all honesty they must admit with Paul that their

generosity does not begin to compare with the generosity of God who has provided most abundantly in the past and will continue to do so. God's children are the constant and continuous objects of his loving care.

One beautiful spring day, one of my children, then still small, was riding his tricycle near my study window. Suddenly I heard a cry of dismay. What had happened? A wheel of his tricycle had come off.

About to go to his assistance, I saw him hold up the wheel and say to a neighbor walking by, "Mister, can you fix this for me?" I also heard the reply, "Son, I would be glad to but I'm in a hurry. Just ask your Dad, I'm sure he will help you." The answer to that was: "My Dad is a preacher; he can't fix anything."

Well, that happens. Many things are beyond our power or ability. And sometimes we do not even care. But that is never true of God. His Word teaches and our experience confirms that he can do all things.

Come to the Lord's Table with the words of David in mind:

> One thing God has spoken,
>   two things have I heard:
> that you, O God, are strong
>   and that you, O Lord, are loving.
>   (Ps. 62:11, 12)

Divine Sufficiency

Read the text carefully: not "out of" but "according to his glorious riches in Christ Jesus." There is a difference. Perhaps an illustration will help us understand.

Someone solicits from you a contribution for a worthy cause. You are in a position to make a generous donation but because you are preoccupied, and your billfold and checkbook are "not handy," you give the few coins you happen to have in your pocket. That means you gave, but you gave "out of your riches," not "according to." Is that not what Jesus censured when he noticed the rich giving to the temple treasury "out of their wealth" while a poor widow "out of her poverty put in all she had to live on" (Luke 21:4).

God never gives in a thoughtless or miserly manner. He gives according to his glorious riches. Those are the riches of his grace merited for us by Christ by his sacrifice on the cross, and poured out on us when he rose and became our ascended Lord.

The riches of glory become our possession and experience through Christ. We not only receive them from the Father through Christ as mediator but they are ours through union and fellowship with him. Through the Spirit dwelling in our hearts we are in Christ and Christ is in us.

Does this sound too good to be true; that God will meet all our needs? Not at all. What the Word teaches and the Lord's Supper confirms is ours, and the central theme of the message is salvation for sinners, infinite grace for believers. Justified, we are sanctified; and sanctified, we are glorified!

Grace beyond measure:

> It is revealed in God's word.
> We see it in the cross.
> It is shed abroad in our hearts.
> We experience it every day.
> It transforms our lives.
>
> Marvelous grace of our loving Lord,
>   Grace that exceeds our sin and our guilt,
> Yonder on Calvary's mount outpoured,
>   There where the blood of the Lamb was spilt.

Dark is the stain that we cannot hide;
  What can avail to wash it away?
Look there is flowing a crimson tide;
  Whiter than snow you may be today.

Grace, grace, God's grace
  Grace that will pardon and cleanse within;
Grace, grace, God's grace,
  Grace that is greater than all our sin.

                              Julia H. Johnston

18

The Great "I Am"

> *God said to Moses, "I am who I am. This is what you are to say to the Israelites. 'I am has sent me to you'"* (Exod. 3:14).

A. **The Setting**
   1. Moses called to deliver Israel from Egypt
      a) Fearful of his own limitations
      b) Fearful of his reception
   2. God reveals himself
      a) The holy, exalted God
      b) The God of the burning bush
      c) The God of wondrous mercy
   3. The God of the covenant
B. **The Meaning**
   1. The eternal, unchanging God
   2. The eternally faithful God
C. **New Testament Enrichment**
   1. Jesus' declaration
   2. Jesus' sevenfold claims
D. **Our Response**
   1. Confessing need of grace and gratitude for grace
   2. Trusting in Christ's fullness
   3. Vowing humble service

Standing on Horeb, the mountain of God, Moses is fearful, and he has reason to be. He has just been commissioned by God to bring the Israelites out of Egypt. He must leave his shepherd's task, to which he has long grown accustomed, and return to the land from which he had fled for his life because he had killed an Egyptian forty years before. What if someone should recognize him?

Moses has other misgivings. By this time the Israelites have forgotten him. Will they receive him as a spokesman and deliverer sent from God?

Furthermore, the task assigned to him seems impossible because of his own limitations and because Pharaoh will block his attempt to rescue the Israelites from their enslavement.

Understandably Moses demurs; he raises serious objections. He has not volunteered for this assignment and he refuses to be drafted. He considers himself inadequate and unqualified.

From a strictly human point of view he is justified. But that is the wrong perspective. He does not go alone; it is God who through him will perform this mighty deed. Moses must put all his trust in the greatness of God. For encouragement Moses is given a remarkable revelation of who God is and what he is like—a revelation which climaxes in this statement of five one-syllable words, "I am who I am."

The Setting

Look for a moment at the setting of that simple but majestic statement, that its meaning may be indelibly imprinted on our minds and may forever fortify our faith.

Moses is tending his sheep when, unexpectedly, on Mount Horeb God "appeared to him in flames of fire from within a bush. Moses saw that though the bush was on fire it did not burn up" (Exod. 3:2). Prompted by curiosity, Moses approached to investigate this strange sight but stopped in his tracks when God called to him, "Moses, Moses! . . . Take off your sandals, for the place where you are standing is holy ground" (vs. 5).

God was in the burning bush! The symbolism is tremendously significant. Amid the flames of cruel oppression Israel is threatened with extinction, preserved only by the presence of God in her midst.

In his presence Moses must remove his sandals for this God is holy. He is perfect and pure, in him is no flaw or weakness. But the original word used emphasizes as well that God is exalted far above all creatures on earth and in heaven. He is the sovereign Lord. Let the earth and all men tremble in his presence and let his people trust him without reservation.

In verse seven this God of glory and power reveals that he is also the God of wondrous mercy. Listen: "The Lord said; "I have seen the misery of my people in Egypt, I have heard them crying out because of their slave drivers, and I am concerned about their suffering." Allow me to underscore certain words: *"Misery, suffering, I have seen, I have heard, I am concerned."*

What compassion! God is not indifferent. He is deeply moved with our sufferings and needs. He reaches out with heart and hand. We know that deliverance must and will come.

Notice that God who preserves and saves introduces himself to Moses as the "God of your father, the God of Abraham, the God of Isaac, and the God of Jacob." Abraham, the man of superlative faith; Isaac, Abraham's covenant child;" and Jacob, God's "problem child." With them God had established a covenant, a relationship of love extending to their posterity. He is Israel's God who keeps the covenant he has made, always faithful to his promises and his people.

This God of Israel's deliverance is the God of our salvation. Scripture makes this very clear, "If you belong to Christ, then you are Abraham's seed, and heirs according to the promise" (Gal. 3:29).

The God to whom we belong and with whom we commune is holy and majestic, mighty to save. Were he anything
less salvation would be impossible. Think of his greatness,
glorify his name as you sit at his table or kneel at his feet.

> All lands to God in joyful sounds
> Aloft your voices raise;
> Sing forth the honor of his Name
> And glorious make his praise.
>
> O come, behold the works of God,
> His mighty doings see;
> In dealing with the sons of men
> Most wonderful is he!
>   Versification of Psalm 66

Rejoice in his compassion. He sees, he hears, he is concerned. Remember the words:

> No earthly father loves like thee,
>   No mother half so mild,
> Bears and forbears as thou has done;
>   With me, thy sinful child.
>   Frederick W. Faber, 1848

And the blood of the covenant symbolized in the wine
of the Lord's Supper, as Jesus himself said, is meant to
deepen our assurance of God's faithfulness and love as we
sit at the Lord's Table and focus our full attention on the
cross.

The Meaning

Having considered the setting, look at the meaning of the
words "I am who I am." They provide a wealth of truth
and comfort.

First of all, the expression "I am who I am" means that God is eternal and unchangeable. What a contrast to earth and men, to ourselves and what we see all around us! Israel's situation appeared hopeless and Moses was preoccupied with his shortcomings.

But God, eternal and immutable, is not restricted or hindered in carrying out his eternal plan, his promises of grace. His power is never decreased; his love never diminished. He is all-sufficient in himself and for his people.

There is in those words, "I am who I am" also a deeper thought: God, eternal and unchangeable, is unchangeable in his faithfulness. He preserves his people and keeps his promises. Have no fear; what he says he will do, and those he loves he will never forsake.

This thought is emphasized for Moses by God himself in preparation for the challenge to be faced on his arrival in Egypt. Notice the dialogue that takes place:

> Moses said to God, "Suppose I go to the Israelites and say to them, "The God of your fathers has sent me to you, and they ask me, 'What is his name?' Then what shall I tell them?

> God said to Moses, "I am who I am. This is what you are to say to the Israelites: 'I AM has sent me to you.' "

> God also said to Moses, "Say to the Israelites, 'The Lord, the God of your fathers—the God of Abraham, the God of Isaac and the God of Jacob—has sent me to you.' This is my name forever, the name by which I am to be remembered from generation to generation" (Exod. 3:13–15).

More than four hundred years ago God had predicted Israel's bondage but had also promised deliverance. He tests and tries His people, but never forgets or leaves them in the lurch. Think of the millions in this world who depend on deities that do not hear and cry out to gods who cannot answer!

New Testament Enrichment

For us these words "I am who I am" have been given fuller and richer meaning in New Testament revelation. Jesus identified himself as the incarnation of the eternal unchangeable God when he said, "I tell you the truth, before Abraham was born, I am!" (John 8:58). Behold your eternally faithful God who, in the fullness of time, sent his Son to save us from sin. And remember: "Jesus Christ is the same, yesterday and today and forever" (Heb. 13:8).

But to appreciate the depth of meaning in the great "I Am" for our faith and life turn your thoughts to the sevenfold claim of Jesus as recorded in the Gospel of John:

"I am the bread of life" (John 6:35).

"I am the light of the world" (8:12).

"I am the gate [the door]" (10:9).

"I am the good shepherd" (10:11).

"I am the resurrection and the life" (11:25).

"I am the way, the truth, and the life (14:6).

"I am the true vine" (15:1).

O what plenitude of truth and grace given us in Christ—the supreme message of divine love for sinners and saints, for all who repent and believe! You have no need God cannot fulfill, "earth has no sorrows, that heaven cannot heal." Hear the message of the Lord's Supper, look to the cross, remember and believe that Christ died for the complete remission of all our sins. "He who did not spare his own Son, but gave him up for us all—how will he not also, along with him, graciously give us all things?" (Rom. 8:32).

Our Response

In response to the majestic "I am" of God and the beautifully interpretive claims of Jesus we ask ourselves: who am I? Are we all agreed on this personal confession? Lord,

I am only one of the countless creatures on earth dependent on your care.

I am one of all the many sinners who need your grace.

I am one of the lost who seek you in faith.

I am one of those erring saints who need forgiveness and mercy.

I am one of those pleading Christians who cry out in mercy and great need.

I am one of those fearful children whose hope is in you.

I am one of those saved by grace who lift their hearts in grateful praise.

I am "little me" but I dare to sing:

> Plenteous grace with thee is found,
>   Grace to cover all my sin;
> Let the healing streams abound,
>   Make me, keep me, pure within.
> Thou of life the fountain art,
>   Freely let me take of thee;
> Spring thou up within my heart,
>   Rise to all eternity.
>   Charles Wesley, 1740

Again, I am "little me" humbly and gratefully confessing:

> I am only one,
> But still I am me
> I cannot do everything,
> But still I can do something;
> And because I cannot do everything
> I will not refuse to do something that I can do.
>   Edward Everett Hale

19

The Royal Family

> *Now Jesus' mother and brothers came to see him, but they were not able to get near him because of the crowd. Someone told him, "Your mother and brothers are standing outside, waiting to see you."*
> *He replied, "My mother and brothers are those who hear God's Word and put it into practice"* (Luke 8:19–21).

A. Jesus Family
   1. A loving relationship
   2. Their manifest concern for Jesus
   3. Jesus' strange reaction
B. His Spiritual Family
   1. Has priority over natural family
   2. Consistent with Scripture
      a) In Old Testament—Israel
      b) In New Testament—Church
C. Requirements for Membership
   1. Hear the word of God
   2. Practice the word of God
D. Blessings Enjoyed
   1. Fellowship with God
   2. Fellowship with believers

Jesus' Family

We wonder why Jesus' mother and brothers came to see him. On Mary's part it certainly must have been an indi-

cation of deep love. He was very special. He was her first-
born, he had never given her any trouble, and deep in her
heart she cherished the message she had received from God
even before Jesus' birth: "He will be great and will be called
the Son of the Most High" (Luke 1:32).

And now exciting things were happening. Jesus had left
Nazareth and was deeply involved in his public ministry.
Crowds came to hear him preach and to observe the miracles he performed. In fact when his family arrived at the
place where he ministered the crowd was so great they
could not get near him.

Had they come to enjoy and share in his popularity?
That is unlikely since John in his Gospel informs us, "For
even his own brothers did not believe in him" (John 7:5).
Perhaps they were perturbed by the report that many were
saying of Jesus, "He is demon-possessed and raving mad.
Why listen to him?" (John 10:20).

Be that as it may, we are stung by what appears to be a
very cold reception. Informed of their presence, Jesus did
not go out to meet them but took the occasion to state the
words, "My mother and brothers are those who hear God's
word and put it into practice." We find them startling, completely out of character, but on examination they teach a
valuable lesson.

We know that Jesus appreciated his family. In Luke 2:51
we are told that as a child he accompanied Joseph and
Mary to Nazareth "and was obedient to them." After his
soul-stirring experience in the temple at the age of twelve,
he returned to Nazareth for almost two decades of service,
obedience, and obscurity. When the appointed-time arrived
he would reveal who he was and what he had come to do.
In the meantime he lived in close fellowship with his family.

And it could well be that Jesus had special responsibilities
to his family during this period. We notice that Luke makes
no mention of Joseph's presence, only Jesus' mother and

brothers. For what reason? Was he too busy or, as is more likely, had Joseph died? If so, had Jesus, the oldest son become the main support of the family? Was it his sweat that provided their bread?

We cannot believe that Jesus held aloof from his family because he did not care. His family certainly was not excluded from his heart, a heart with room for others who sought him.

His Spiritual Family

Actually, Jesus responded as he did because he chose this occasion to teach a truth which his family and all others must learn.

What is that lesson? Simply this: though family ties and physical relationships are precious, imparting richer and fuller meaning to life, they must be superseded by spiritual ties. The bond of faith and love which unites us to Christ is the most significant relationship in life. Could Jesus have expressed it more emphatically than he did when he stated in another connection, "Anyone who loves his father or mother more than me is not worthy of me; anyone who loves his son or daughter more than me is not worthy of me" (Matt. 10:37).

Sinners reconciled to God in Jesus Christ are members of the royal family, not of an earthly domain, but of the eternal heavenly kingdom of God. As sons and daughters of God they are the nobility of both earth and heaven, not because of their inherent goodness or recognized superiority but because of divine grace. Is there a greater honor or privilege that can come to any man than to be a child of God?

This is the truth Jesus intended to drive home. Mary and his brothers, favored as they are by his relationship to them, must learn to know him as their Savior and Lord. Such union with him brings supreme and eternal blessedness.

This emphasis on the gracious and glorious relationship between God and his people is found in all of Scripture. God established his covenant with Abraham and his seed; he constantly referred to Israel as "My people," "My chosen;" and in the New Testament we are specifically told that believers are "members of God's household" (Eph. 2:19).

The climax of this comforting truth is found in the Book of Revelation where John sees the new heaven and earth, "the Holy City, the new Jerusalem, coming down out of heaven from God" and hears a loud voice from the throne saying, "Now the dwelling of God is with men, and he will live with them. They will be his people, and God himself will be with them and be their God" (Rev. 21:2, 3). The promise to Abraham, to Israel, and the church, has reached final fulfillment.

And as we look to Jesus, remembering his death on the cross and anticipating his glorious return, we sing:

> My Father's own Son, the Savior of men,
>   Once wandered o'er earth as the poorest of them;
> But now he is reigning forever on high
>   And will give me a home in heaven by and by.
>
> I once was an outcast stranger on earth
>   A sinner by choice, and an alien by birth!
> But I've been adopted, my name's written down,
>   An heir to a mansion, a robe, and a crown.
>
> I'm the child of a King, The child of a King!
>   With Jesus, my Savior, I'm the child of a King.
>   John B. Sumner

Requirements for Membership

Who are these believers? How can the members of the royal family be identified? Who are Jesus' brothers and sisters? In the chapter text they are clearly identified by Jesus himself: "My mother and brothers are those who hear God's Word and put it into practice."

Jesus was not deceived by the crowds who have come to listen. He knew that when he did not accommodate himself to their expectations and proclaimed what they do not want to hear they would turn away. Spiritual transformation is experienced only by those who hear the word of God and then put it into practice. Such are brought from darkness to light, from poverty to riches, from sin to salvation, from death to life.

In one of his parables, the parable of the sower, Jesus indicated that men hear the word of God in various ways, but only one way is acceptable and effective: — the way of faith. Men must hear with the heart, a heart made responsive by the Spirit to the Word he himself has inspired. Only then do they experience the saving power of the gospel. Our faith must be genuine.

But how can we tell? Especially for those of us who have been exposed to the gospel and been members of the church for many years that question preys on our minds. We have grown accustomed to our spirituality and sometimes wonder if our faith and commitment are real. Yes, we should examine ourselves.

Jesus says that hearing the Word must go hand in hand with practice of the Word; that is the basic test we should apply to our faith. Genuine faith manifests itself in obedience. Unbelief and faith are both known by the fruit they bear. In Psalm 1 it is said of the righteous man:

> He is like a tree planted by streams of water,
>   which yields its fruit in season . . . (Ps 1:3).

And this same truth is expressed by Jesus in a striking analogy:

No good tree bears bad fruit, nor does a bad tree bear good fruit. Each tree is recognized by its own fruit. People do not pick figs from thornbushes or grapes from briers. The good man brings good things out of the good stored up in his heart, and the evil man brings evil things out of the evil stored up in his heart. For out of the overflow of his heart his mouth speaks. (Luke 6:43 – 45)

To examine our hearts is not easy, although if we are honest with ourselves, we know what our basic commitment is: to the world and our sinful self, or to Christ. But if you have difficulty assessing the deepest desire of your heart, look at your life. Can you see there the fruits of faith even though they are not as bountiful and beautiful as they ought to be?

Remember:

Christianity is a religion.

Christianity is a relationship.

Christianity is a confession.

Christianity is a life.

Regrettably our Christian confession is marred by many divisions and many inconsistencies. The world pounces on these and individuals use them as an excuse for their lack of interest or response.

We look at ourselves and see much that compromises our Christian confession. In every Christian life there are many unchristian aspects. Do not be discouraged. God welcomes and recognizes us as his own, not because we are perfect, but because we are forgiven and the blood through which we are forgiven is also the blood that cleanses and purifies.

I am reminded of the new convert, a babe in Christ, who

in somewhat illiterate but eloquent fashion said it all when
he exclaimed:

> I ain't what I oughta be.
> I ain't what I wanna be,
> I ain't what I'm gonna be,
> But thank God, I ain't what I was.

So begin where you are, do the best you can, and trust
in the Lord. Someday we shall indeed be perfect, in the
meantime God simply requires that we be faithful. Faithful
in what? In hearing and doing his word.

Blessings Enjoyed

If our relationship to God in Christ is the most important
relationship in life and if this means that we must hear and
practice the word of God in all sincerity, it is also reason
for the greatest joy. It brings untold and inestimable blessings for we are members of his family.

That immediately suggests a wonderful fellowship, the
fellowship of love. We experience blessing in his love for us
and in our love for him. Increasingly we realize what he
means to us. We sing:

> Jesus is all the world to me,
> My life, my joy, my all;
> He is my strength from day to day,
> Without him I would fall.
> When I am sad, to him I go,
> No other one can cheer me so;
> When I am sad he makes me glad,
> He's my friend.
>   Will L. Thompson

And this fellowship with God is the basis of believers'
fellowship with one another. If we love God we love his

children. The family of God should be the most closely-knit family on earth. Jesus gave us the new commandment that we should love one another as he loved us and John, the apostle of love, tells us:

> We love because he first loved us. If anyone says, "I love God," yet hates his brother, he is a liar. For anyone who does not love his brother, whom he has seen, cannot love God, whom he has not seen. And he has given us this command: Whoever loves God must also love his brother" (1 John 4:19–21).

Now it is true that such love remains an ideal which we have not fully attained. Even in the upper room, when about to celebrate the Passover and the Lord's Supper, the disciples of Jesus disputed with one another as to who would be the greatest in the kingdom. And when Jesus washed their feet because they refused to perform such menial service it was evident they had much to learn about the meaning and practice of Christian love. The epistles of Paul make frequent reference to pride and selfishness and disunity in the church. He found it necessary to admonish believers again and again.

But when these faults are admitted they do not warrant the conclusion that love is not present. Brotherly love and the communion of saints may be lacking not absent. Members of the congregation, and pastors especially, know how it is practiced and experienced, even though imperfectly.

Members of the congregation do work and worship together in the unity of faith, hope, and love. They do confess their sins and forgive the sins of others. They do rejoice with those who rejoice and weep with those who weep. All the beautiful people in the kingdom are not in heaven, they are with us on earth.

What a glorious family. All races, colors, and backgrounds, from all classes of men and all stages in life, a constantly growing family of those who are born again and thus are born or adopted into the family of God.

We enjoy a meal much more when we enjoy it with others. The Lord's Supper is served family style. In communion with God we have fellowship with one another.

Think of it, members of the same family with Abraham, Moses, David, Isaiah, Paul, and all the saints, many of whom have remained anonymous. Did not Jesus teach that the last should be first and the least would be the greatest in the kingdom of God? But best of all we are children of God, brothers and sisters in Christ.

Come let us feast and fellowship together in and with the Lord.

20

Divine Encouragement

Take heart, son; your sins are forgiven (Matt. 9:2).

Take courage! It is I, Don't be afraid (Matt. 14:27).

But take heart! I have overcome the world (John 16:33).

A. Sins Forgiven
   1. Our physical needs are great
   2. Our spiritual needs are greater
   3. Jesus is the answer
B. Christ's Presence
   1. The answer to our fears
   2. Assured in his Word
   3. Enjoyed by faith
C. Victory Assured
   1. The dangers are real
   2. Discouragement is prevalent
   3. We shall triumph
      a) Christ has gained the victory
      b) In that victory we share

A high school teacher, highly respected as a teacher and as a man of God, used the above texts for a chapel meditation a few days after he had observed an athletic contest and had appreciated the efforts of cheerleaders and spectators to urge their team on to victory. He used the

King James Version, where in each instance the admonition of Jesus is translated: "Be of good cheer."

Accommodating himself to his youthful audience he chose as his theme, "Three Cheers." He emphasized the encouragement given us by God, and evidently the thought left a lasting impression. Even during his retirement former students indicated that they remembered that chapel — a real tribute to the man and his message, a tribute always humbly received.

Is there anyone, even among God's children, who does not need encouragement? Some may deny the fact, but we know that encouragement must come from God. He gives comfort, strength, and hope. When we open God's word, when we turn to God in prayer, when we gather at the Lord's Table, we do so with a deep sense of need. Without that need, heavenly fellowship will not be found.

Consider briefly these heartening statements of Jesus intended to impart strength and inspiration.

Sins Forgiven

"Take heart, son; your sins are forgiven."

Friends carried a paralytic to Jesus. The man's need was great, he was completely dependent. People were willing and able to help him but none could heal him. Jesus of Nazareth, who had performed miraculous deeds was his only hope for recovery of health and strength. Jesus responded to an earnest, hopeful expression of faith by commanding the paralytic to rise, and "the man got up and went home."

What an unbelievable transformation! People were astonished and it would take this man days and weeks to comprehend what had really happened to him. And even then he would not fully understand. Is there anything Jesus cannot do?

But the healing of this man was prefaced by Jesus' statement, "Take heart, son; your sins are forgiven." What a lesson for that occasion and for believers in every age!

Though our physical needs are great, our spiritual needs are greater. To be sure, it is a blessing to be strong and healthy. It is also a blessing to live long, provided, of course, that we are well enough to enjoy it. But that does not compare with the never-ending life in fellowship with God.

Our most serious problem is the malady of sin, our estrangement from God, and our tendency to do what is contrary to his will or to leave undone what he requires as an expression of obedience and gratitude. How can we overcome? Only by the grace of God, only through Jesus Christ, our Savior.

"Blessed is he whose transgressions are forgiven, whose sins are covered" (Ps. 32:1). This is the message Jesus brings, the blessing he bestows.

We know one another, we associate together, enjoy mutual fellowship, but the man or woman next to you at the Lord's Supper cannot read your mind and know all that is in your heart. And that is good. Some things do not belong in the public arena of life.

Is it not true that we are more expressive concerning the good things than the bad? I mean those that are very personal. A good report card causes a child to hasten home to share the happiness, but a poor one results in a slow, lingering pace because parents and family must be included in the disappointment. A husband would much rather return home to his wife with the news that he has received a promotion rather than share the distressing fact that he has lost his job.

And so we frequently keep our burdens to ourselves. Others do not know the burden you bear, the heartache you endure, the temptations with which you struggle, the hidden tears you shed. But God knows. To him our lives are an open book.

Does not this instance of the healing of the paralytic serve as a reminder? Jesus knew this man's need far better than those who were spectators of this remarkable event; he saw the burden more clearly than the helpful friends who brought him to Jesus; he comprehended the man's condition with greater understanding than that of the man himself. Jesus saw more than the outward circumstance. He saw the struggle and distress in this man's soul. Even more than help for his body, he needed healing for his spirit.

The burden of sin is unbearable. Sooner or later it will crush and destroy. We are afflicted with a malady not curable by medication or surgery. Only God can take away our sin.

Yes, we believe in the forgiveness of sins. It is the teaching of Scripture and our confession.

But why is it that we hesitate to appropriate that wonder of grace for ourselves and are lacking in the assurance and joy that our personal transgressions are forgiven?

Remember, forgiveness is for all who repent and believe — for others and also for us. Did not Jesus say, "Son, your sins are forgiven"? If we come to him confessing our sin and guilt, we will hear him say it to us. Your sorrow shall be turned to joy. Jesus saves! There is power in the blood!

Christ's Presence

"Take courage! It is I. Don't be afraid."

The disciples were in a boat on the Sea of Galilee. That was not unusual and they were calm and confident. But when a threatening storm arose, they feared for their lives.

Then to their consternation they saw, a form they believed to be a ghost walking toward them. What to do?

Before they could decide the answer to that question, to which there really was no answer, Jesus identified himself. Above the tumult of wind and wave they heard him say, "Take courage! It is I. Don't be afraid."

Smooth sailing on the sea of life? Sometimes, but certainly not always. God's children are not immune to danger and hardship. We cannot foresee the extent and intensity of the sufferings we may have to endure. And for that we may be grateful.

Scripture is not silent concerning the suffering of the saints. All around us we see evidence of pain. Although we are on the sea with Jesus:

> Still the storms arise.
> Still we are afraid.
> Still we need his care.

Although it is only natural to be most concerned about our own situation, we may not become preoccupied with it. Rather it should cause us to grow in our sympathy for others.

And we should learn to trust more completely in the providence of God and the presence of our Savior. He will not allow us to drift beyond his love and care. Guided by his wisdom we are protected by his power.

"Be not afraid!" An admonition which sounds like a command. It also sounds very foolish. The disciples were veteran sailors battling contrary winds and stormy waves. They knew when to be concerned. When a mysterious figure walks toward them, is it not foolish to tell them not to be afraid when they are sure they see a ghost? What would you and I have done? What would we have felt?

It is true that the words of Jesus did not seem realistic. They seem to ignore the actual situation, the frightening circumstances. The apostle Paul in one of his epistles even refers to "the foolishness of preaching." Does the message of Scripture really fit our situation?

Many people are forceful, even vociferous, in their denial. They put their trust in themselves and in the things they can see, not in a God who is invisible and, in their minds, does not even exist. It is up to us, they say, to row our own boat and if it capsizes, we either sink or swim.

Where do we find strength to endure the suffering that seems unendurable? When faith falters, what can keep it alive? The answer is in Jesus Christ, who says to us as he said to his disciples, "Take courage! It is I. Don't be afraid." The assurance of his abiding presence brings the comfort that we are in his care.

This story illustrates that truth: A little girl whose mother had to attend a meeting at church, was left in her father's care for the evening. Of course he received a few instructions: Read her a story or two, give her a snack, and put her to bed at eight o'clock. You wonder how things turned out?

Well, the father did very well. He did as told and had his little daughter in bed five minutes ahead of schedule. There was a reason, his favorite magazine had arrived that day.

Absorbed in his reading, he thought he heard a sound. After listening a moment he decided he had been wrong. Then it happened again. This time he listened longer and more intently. Then he heard his daughter calling "Daddy." When he asked, "What is it?" she cheerfully replied, "Oh, nothing, I just wanted to know if you were still there." Likewise, so we need to know the presence of our Lord.

And why should we doubt? Did not Jesus say, "For where two or three come together in my name, there am I with them" (Matt. 18:20)? He is with us in church, with us at the Lord's Table, with us wherever we go and wherever we are. Always and everywhere He is near.

We have double assurance, for in addition to the promise

just referred to he, at the time of his ascension to heaven, left with his disciples and us this blessed assurance of his presence: "And surely I will be with you always, to the very end of the age" (Matt. 28:20). He is with us always; he is with us now.

Victory Assured

"But take heart! I have overcome the world."

Three cheers! Divine encouragement, the assurance of forgiveness, the comfort of his presence, and the guarantee of victory.

When Jesus spoke to his disciples about his impending departure and of the ordeals that awaited them on the road ahead, they were disturbed. The prospect of separation and danger created fear and anxiety.

From our perspective many years later, we probably have a clearer conception of Jesus' predictions. We have witnessed most of their fulfillment. God's children have been persecuted; demonic and human forces have assailed the church. Living in a violent world, we suffer along with others, and believers in Christ are subjected to additional oppression for Christ's sake.

But the church will continue, she shall never be eradicated. She is the Lord's precious possession and he keeps her in the hollow of his almighty hand. Nevertheless there are times when we are vexed by doubts and fears.

And as individual believers we wonder sometimes how we can continue to live in or live at all. When our situation appears desperate we are tempted to despair. With the saints of old in time of tribulation we ask, "Where is God?" Is there any hope of rescue?

Why do we so frequently underestimate God and fail to find security in his promises? Though we have faith, it is not always as strong and vibrant as it ought to be.

Then we need to look to him who has been where we are and for whom the suffering was greater and the battle more fierce than any in which we have been or shall ever be involved. And did he succumb? No, he gained victory for himself and his cause. And in that victory we are included.

He has met the enemy—his and ours. And the outcome was never in doubt for even before he was crucified, and before he rose again and ascended into heaven, He said: "But take heart! I have overcome the world."

Does the devil encourage doubt and fear? Does your conscience accuse you so that misgivings well up in your soul? Then look away from yourself. Come to Jesus just as you are and see that he who suffered and died for you on the cross is now Lord of lords, and King of kings. He has conquered sin, death, and the grave; and even Satan himself, His victory insures our triumph. His glory is the guarantee of ours.

Rejoice, then, in the divine encouragement revealed in the Word and sealed in the sacrament. Our sins are forgiven, we dwell in God's presence, and we shall overcome.

21

Answer to a Pleading Cry

> *O Lord, listen! O Lord, forgive! O Lord, hear and act! For your sake, O my God, do not delay, because your city and your people bear your Name* (Dan. 9:19).

A. The Suppliant
1. Daniel, a man of prayer
2. Moved by divine revelation
3. Concerned about the plight of God's people
4. Pleading with his entire being

B. The Supplication
1. O Lord, listen
2. O Lord, forgive
3. O Lord, hear and do

C. The Sequel
1. Immediate assurance
2. God will glorify himself, that he is heard
3. Israel shall be returned to the promised land
4. Final deliverance thorugh the promised Messiah

The Suppliant

The first thing that claims our attention as we read this concluson of Daniel's prayer is the intensity, the urgency, of his petition. This is truly a prayer of supplication. It arises from the depths of Daniel's soul; it involves his entire being. He is intent on God. There was reason for such a pleading cry.

We know that Daniel, characterized in Scripture as a man of unusual consecration and courage, was a man of prayer. Fellowship with God was the secret of his loyalty and devotion.

When at the instigation of his administrators and advisors King Darius issued a decree against anyone who during the next thirty days prayed to any god other than himself, Daniel defied the king and went home to his upstairs room where the windows were opened toward Jerusalem. "Three times a day he got down on his knees and prayed, giving thanks to God, just as he had done before" (Dan. 6:10).

He was not foolhardy and reckless; he was fearless. He had no intention of parading his piety but neither was he inclined to compromise his confession. His faith in God was greater than his fear of the king. Now he offers a very special prayer and we are privileged to hear his impassioned plea.

The specific occasion for this prayer is the vision Daniel had been given concerning the years ahead as the angel Gabriel had been instructed to tell him: "Son of man, understand that the vision concerns the time of the end" (Dan. 18:17). But that outline of future events affected Daniel in this manner: "I, Daniel, was exhausted and lay ill for several days. Then I got up and went about the king's business. I was appalled by the vision; it was beyond understanding" (Dan. 8:27).

In that situation Daniel unburdened himself to the Lord. And he need not hesitate. God is ready and eager to answer "emergency prayers" provided that is not the only time we pray. We cannot manage without him. You may be sure that God was expecting Daniel to kneel at his throne.

Daniel was a spokesman for God to a people in exile. They were being chastened for their waywardness and disobedience. Daniel had no quarrel with that. He did not question the justice of God, but his heart bled because of the severe nature and long duration of Israel's trial. He prays because he must. His compulsion is the compulsion of love. These people are his people. When they hurt, he hurts; when they weep, he weeps.

We arrive at a better understanding of the urgency in the prophet's petition. We sympathize with his pleading cry: "O Lord, listen! O Lord, forgive! O Lord, hear and act! O my God, do not delay. . . ."

In his extremity Daniel calls on the only one who can help and by example invites Israel to do the same. Whether they join him or not, whether or not they are ready to turn unto the Lord, he will intercede on their behalf. God who has been their help in ages past is their hope for years to come.

The preceding verses describe what the Lord meant to Daniel. Listen to him as he addresses God:

O Lord, the great and awesome God, who keeps his covenant of love with all who love him and obey his commands . . . (Dan. 9:4).

Lord you are righteous . . . (Dan. 9:7).

Now, O Lord our God, who brought your people out of Egypt with a mighty hand and who made for yourself a name that endures to this day . . . (Dan. 9:15).

Surely the God of heaven who has made a covenant with his people on earth, that God who is faithful, just, and merciful, the God of deliverance, is able to answer prayer and will show His mercy anew. He will never forsake his people in distress. He will demonstrate as he has done before that he is the God of salvation.

You may have read the little book by J. B. Phillips entitled *Your God Is Too Small* (MacMillan, 1953). He is correct in exposing our concept of God as being altogether too limited. God is greater than we know, greater than we think, greater than we imagine.

Humbly, expectantly we draw near to him in Christ; sit with him at the table he has prepared. We kneel in spirit before him exalted in highest heaven and yet as near to us as our hands and feet. We breathe the prayer, and every syllable is a cry of both our need and our faith.

> May all those who seek thee, and make thee their
> choice,
> Great gladness and blessedness see;
> May all those who love thy salvation rejoice
> And constantly magnify thee.
>
> I cry in deep need and thy help I implore;
> Make haste to my rescue, I pray;
> My Savior thou art and my strength evermore,
> No longer thy coming delay.
>
> Versification of Psalm 10

The Supplication

Daniel prays for a blessing on the people of Israel. He sees their plight and is deeply stirred by their need. Though in the providence of God he has enjoyed special privileges and advantages as a reward for steadfast courage and faith, he has not grown aloof from his people, so long and painfully oppressed that they are inclined to despair. He identifies with them and prays for the dawning of a brighter day. His personal trials may be over but he cannot be happy until the ordeal for his people also comes to an end.

It is impossible for this man of God to give full expression to his thoughts, let alone his feelings. He can only do his best, trusting and believing the Lord will understand.

Who can listen to this stirring climax of Daniel's prayer without being deeply moved? And if that is so, can you conceive of any divine indifference? We are positive the prayer will be heard. We know that the surest thing about prayer is this: God answers it.

We hesitate to analyze this petition for fear it may lose some of its luster. Why run the risk of spoiling it by leaving our fingermarks? And yet, we must seek to understand the spirit and context of this prayer; we want to make it our own. We are going to need it—very likely, again and again.

"O Lord, listen!" Is God slow to hear or reluctant to pay attention? Not at all. Prayer is not overcoming God's resistance, it is laying hold of God's willingness.

But for his own comfort Daniel must be assured that he has the Lord's full and undivided attention. He is praying not simply for himself but for a people in such misery and peril that their very survival seems to be at stake. He cannot watch that nation die. And in his heart he knows God will not allow that to happen.

On the other hand, he knows that Israel by terrible and continued transgression has forfeited the right to receive special treatment from God. The Lord has been faithful but his people have not walked in the way of the covenant. If they are left to themselves and if the Lord does not intervene, who can they blame? Not God, only themselves.

So Daniel pleads for mercy. The prophet who has been God's spokesman to the people now becomes their spokesman before God. He pleads for mercy, first of all this mercy—that God will lend a listening ear and hear their distressful, pleading cry.

"O Lord, forgive!" In this ardent communion with God there is no attempt whatsoever to shift the blame. Daniel confesses that God is just. The chastening the Lord sent had been deserved. The people are guilty and Daniel himself is guilty along with them. Why should God listen to them?

Sorrow for sin is the first step toward the experience of forgiveness. God who is just is also merciful. He is a forgiving God and has revealed himself as such in his pleadings and promises. But to have the assurance in our souls that our sin is not an insurmountable barrier between us and God, to know that the problem has been solved, we must turn to God in penitence and faith. Moved by the Spirit we must move; we must reach out in faith for proffered grace. And receiving it we find joy and peace.

The poet, Robert Southey has expressed it so well:

> Lord, who art merciful as well as just,
> Incline thine ear to me, a child of dust.
> Not what I would, O Lord, I offer thee,
>   Alas! but what I can.
> Father Almighty, who has made me man
> And bade me look to heaven, for thou art there
> Accept my sacrifice and humble prayer:
>   Four things, which are in thy treasury
> I lay before thee, Lord, with this petition:
> My nothingness, my wants, my sin, and my
>   contrition.

So we must pray. Plead with God for forgiveness. We have sinned. We must assume our share of responsibility for the sins of our nation, for faults and failures in the church, and we must acknowledge the evil in our own hearts. Remember that in the parable of Jesus it was the publican, not the Pharisee, who "went home justified before God" (Luke 18:14).

The Lord's Supper reminds us of the warning, "If we claim to be without sin, we deceive ourselves and the truth is not in us" (1 John 1:8).

But the Lord's Supper also offers blessed assurance, "If we confess our sins, he is faithful and just and will forgive us our sins and purify us from all unrighteousness" (1 John 1:9). Inherent in divine pardon is the prospect of perfection. We are destined for glory.

"O Lord, hear and act." Daniel realizes that the situation he faces is beyond his and Israel's control. Only God can redeem and rectify. And He will! The Lord God who rescued their fathers, and who during their present exile has demonstrated to Israel and her enemies his sovereign authority, is never at a loss for power and is able to deliver.

With holy longing, we might almost say impatience, Daniel cries out for the day of emancipation. He calls for God to set them free.

When we experience forgiveness and final assurance of it in the Word and sacrament we thank God for the cross and eagerly await the crown. We will pray and persevere until our Savior comes. And in the interval, while we are deeply disturbed by all the sin and suffering in this world, we have also caught a glimpse of the celestial serenity that lies ahead and we pray: Come, Lord Jesus, Come quickly.

The Sequel

Daniel believes that God will listen and forgive, that God does hear, and that he must forgive. Is that not irreverent? Not really! As you examine his petition you notice that he pleads on this basis, ". . . your people bear your Name." The honor of God is involved for he has committed himself by his promises. His people shall prevail; their enemies shall be thwarted. If not, God has failed. That must not and cannot happen.

For that very reason Daniel's prayer receives an immediate response. He tells us, "while I was speaking and praying, confessing my sin and the sin of my people Israel and making request to the Lord my God for his holy hill — while I was still in prayer, Gabriel the man I had seen in the earlier vision, came to me in swift flight . . . and said to me, 'As soon as you began to pray, an answer was given which

I have come to tell you, for you are highly esteemed' "
(Dan. 9:21, 23).

What was the answer? First of all he was given enlightenment as to God's purpose and plan for Israel. It is a message
of comfort and hope. That plan finds fulfillment in Israel's
return to the Promised Land. Restored to God's favor, they
are set free.

And all this is prophetic of that far greater deliverance
to be accomplished by the promised Messiah. He will do
more than save from the oppression of a foreign, hostile
power; he will save his people from the enslavement and
misery of sin — not only Israel but all who turn to him with
penitent, believing hearts.

That is the message which shall be proclaimed to the
ends of the earth, until the salvation wrought by the Lord
shall find its culmination in the final glorification of believers with Christ their Savior and Lord.

We have heard that message. We have seen the unfolding
of the message Daniel received long ago and that great
prophet of God would join us in the declaration that God
answers our prayers beyond what we ask or think.

Do we need forgiveness and grace? Do we believe God's
promises? Is all our faith and hope directed to Jesus Christ?
Are we seeking and growing in that assurance? Do we find
it in the blood of Jesus Christ, God's Son?

Then have no fear. You are saved — saved forevermore.
And to God be the glory!

22

Glorious Certainties!

Therefore, there is now no condemnation for those who are in Christ Jesus (Rom. 8:1).

"And we know that in all things God works for the good of those who love him, who have been called according to his purpose" (Rom. 8:28).

For I am convinced that neither death nor life, neither angels nor demons, neither the present nor the future, nor any powers, neither height nor depth, nor anything else in all creation, will be able to separate us from the love of God that is in Christ Jesus our Lord" (Rom. 8:38–39).

A. **No Condemnation**
   1. For believers in Christ
   2. Unbelievable, but true
   3. Because Christ bore our sin and guilt
B. **No Frustration**
   1. For Christians
   2. A conviction rooted in
      a) God's plan and purpose in our life
      b) He selects and weaves the pattern
      c) He never contradicts the love expressed in Calvary's cross
C. **No Separation**
   1. In spite of all hardship and opposition
   2. Christ was forsaken on our behalf
   3. All things and creatures are under God's control
   4. We are his eternal possession

Doubtless you have heard it said, and may have said it yourself, "You just can't be sure of anything." Life is full of uncertainties. We wonder what will happen next.

I remember a brief paragraph which was brought to my attention by a college student a few years ago. He was expected to memorize it and I think he wondered why. In summary it said: "We are all like chips of wood on the broad expanse of the ocean. Sometimes we near the shore and then again we are carried far out into the deep. Hither and yon, to and fro; where we come to rest, we do not know."

That is fatalism and therefore quite the opposite of Christian faith. Are we the playthings of time and circumstance? Is there no place to stand, no foundation on which we can build? Is it true that we cannot be sure of anything?

Not at all! That glaring generality stands in direct contrast to the glorious certainties revealed in God's word. Briefly we meditate on three of them as presented by Paul in the surpassingly beautiful and comforting words of Romans 8.

What are those certainties? Here they are: no condemnation, no frustration, no separation. Obviously we cannot look at all the details. We focus on the forest, not on each of the trees.

No Condemnation

Paul uses exceptionally forceful language. He does not speak of disapproval, censure, or discipline; he asserts there is no condemnation.

The word "therefore" links the thought very closely to that which precedes. As you know, in the opening chapter of this epistle he stresses the sinfulness of men, exposes the folly of relying on good works or a "righteousness according to the law" for salvation, and magnifies the grace of God. Like Abraham of old, we are justified by faith.

Now then, says Paul, there is no condemnation for believers in Christ; those who have recognized their depravity and have turned to Christ for deliverance. For them there is no condemnation, no possibility, not even the faintest chance, that they shall be lost.

The reason for that is Christ, the Son of God, who, as the substitute for sinful men, suffered and died for their sins. He took our guilt on himself and endured the punishment we deserved. God in mercy provided that all-sufficient sacrifice, and in his justice will did not visit on us the punishment which Christ already bore.

This is the good news of the gospel, the gospel according to Matthew, Mark, Luke, and John — and the gospel according to Paul.

A former parishioner and very dear saint who served as my secretary for several years called me on the phone one morning. I could tell she was excited. Involved with others in a neighborhood Bible study, she had asked her class what they had learned during the year. A boy of twelve volunteered the answer: "I learned that Jesus came into this world to suffer and die for my sin." That said it all. No wonder my secretary, the boy's teacher, was excited as she exclaimed, "Pastor, that is the whole doctrine of the atonement, isn't it?" And she was right. She had reason to be thrilled. A little boy had grasped the heart of the gospel.

No condemnation! Salvation for those "in Christ Jesus," one of Paul's favorite expressions. What does that mean and how do we know if that applies to us? How can we tell if we are in Christ Jesus?

Four thoughts come to mind from the word of God. You may be able to add others. To be in Christ Jesus means:

To believe in Christ as your personal Savior.

To have fellowship with Christ so that he is the joy and strength of your life.

To possess the Spirit of Christ, who enlightens, leads, comforts and sanctifies.

To live for Christ in obedient and cheerful service.

Are we troubled? Do we lack assurance in our confession of faith? Sometimes we reach the mountain-top of conviction and at other times find ourselves in the valley of uncertainty.

We are not alone. Remember that John the Baptist who identified Jesus as the Lamb of God was plagued with doubt when he was imprisoned. And think of the man who, challenged by the statement of Jesus, "Everything is possible for him who believes," was moved to exclaim: "I do believe; help me to overcome my unbelief" (Mark 9:23, 24).

We have reason to be discouraged with ourselves when we see our sin and are troubled by the weakness of our faith. We ask ourselves whether we may come to God and expect forgiveness, whether we may come to the Lord's Supper and expect a blessing.

And the answer is, yes we may, for we come not because we are good but because we know that God is gracious. Hear the invitation:

> Come, ye needy, come and welcome,
>   God's free bounty glorify;
> True belief and true repentance,
>   Every grace that brings you nigh. . . .
> Let not conscience make you linger,
>   Nor of fitness fondly dream;
> All the fitness he requireth
>   Is to feel your need of him.
>   Joseph Hart, 1759

Can you be sure? Yes, you can. "There is no condemnation for those who are in Christ Jesus."

No Frustration

Another glorious certainty: "God works all things for the good of those who love him. . . ."

No frustration? We question that. It is hard to believe. It appears to be contradicted by daily experience. Life is full of disappointments: Expectations unfulfilled, hopes shattered, and plans that go awry. The sea we sail is not always smooth and the road we travel can be very uneven.

But it is nevertheless true that for believers who exercise and cultivate their faith, life is full of contentment and victory. Disappointment is temporary, frustration gives way to confidence and hope. If we love the Lord we must know and do know that he loves us.

Understand then what Paul is saying: All things work together. We must not view experiences in isolation but view them in relationship to God's whole plan for us. We are so shortsighted that we draw unwarranted conclusions. Things that we consider detrimental and mysterious are part of God's gracious plan. They are for our good. It is necessary and wise to watch and wait. Tell me, if life were all roses and no thorns would we feel urgent need of God? How much would we pray?

Our assurance that all things work for good is rooted in God's sovereign purpose and love. He is working out his plan in our lives. We are under his control and progress on the avenue of life under his direction. And since he is our loving Father we must trust him even when we do not understand.

Do children always understand their parents? Of course not. There are times when they are fearful, when they disagree, or even rebel. So, also, we do not always comprehend the ways of our Father in heaven who long ago assured us through the prophet Isaiah:

> "For my thoughts are not your thoughts,
>   neither are your ways, my ways," declares the Lord.
> "As the heavens are higher than the earth,
>   so are my ways higher than your ways
>   and my thoughts than your thoughts."
>
>   (Isa. 55:8, 9)

Often we cannot grasp God's meaning; we misunderstand his intent. We are confused and fearful. We prefer the brighter shades and shy away from the darker colors in the pattern of our lives, only to agree with God at a later date that both were necessary.

> Not till each loom is silent
>   And the shuttles cease to fly,
> Shall God reveal the pattern
>   And explain the reason why.
> The dark threads are as needful
>   In the weaver's skillful hand,
> As the threads of gold and silver
>   For the pattern he had planned.

Isn't it evident that Paul had difficulty with the providence of God in his life? What was his reaction when, called to proclaim the gospel to the Gentile world, he was detained in prison long before the task was finished? It can be imagined that he was ready to climb the walls. But he learned to accept it. As always, God knew what he was doing. He provided Paul with the opportunity to write the message as well as to preach it, that it might be preserved for generations to come. And we are grateful that God in his own way arranged to use this great man of faith to enrich his contemporaries — and also many others, including you and me.

No frustration! Is that an exaggeration? Not when we penetrate to the essence of what Paul is saying. When he insists "that in all things God works for the good of those who love him, who have been called according to his purpose," he is asserting that God never contradicts the love he has expressed for his children on the cross of Calvary. All that he does in our lives is consistent with his grace and our redemption.

All our days are not pleasant. Many experiences in life are very trying. We are not always cheerful, but we can be happy, for we know we are blessed. God's children are never put to shame. Glorious certainty! Come to the Lord confessing your faith and you will grow in assurance of faith.

No Separation

If the Christian life is most rewarding, it is also very demanding. That note is struck by Paul in this very epistle: "Therefore, I urge you, brothers, in view of God's mercy, to offer your bodies as living sacrifices, holy and pleasing to God . . ." (Rom. 12:1). What the apostle preached he also put into practice. His life was such a sacrifice. Indeed Dietrich Bonhoeffer was in accordance biblically when he wrote a book entitled: *The Cost of Discipleship* (tr. by R. H. Fuller. MacMillan Co., 1949).

Paul served faithfully, labored arduously, and suffered many hardships. We wonder how he survived when, in answer to carping critics, he describes his numerous and severe ordeals:

> I have worked much harder, been in prison more frequently, been flogged more severely, and been exposed to death again and again. Five times I received from the Jews the forty lashes minus one. Three times I was beaten with

rods, once I was stoned, three times I was shipwrecked, I spent a night and a day in the open sea, I have been constantly on the move. I have been in danger from rivers, in danger from bandits, in danger from my own country-men, in danger from Gentiles; in danger in the city, in danger in the country, in danger at sea; and in danger from false brothers. I have labored and toiled and have often gone without sleep; I have known hunger and thirst and have gone without food, I have been cold and naked. Be-sides everything else, I face daily the pressure of my con-cern for all the churches.

(2 Cor. 11:23 – 28)

For such service and suffering the Lord selects people very carefully. Many could never stand up under the load Paul had to bear for Christ's sake. He was an extraordinary man, who performed extraordinary service, endured extra-ordinary hardships — for all of which he received extra-ordinary grace.

In this eighth chapter of Romans (vs. 35) Paul recognizes that all believers must bear a cross for Christ's sake and then asks the question: "Who shall separate us from the love of Christ. Shall trouble or hardship or persecution or famine or nakedness or danger or sword?" And the answer to that question given in the text is: Nothing! Absolutely nothing!

Of that Paul is convinced. It is evident that he has revived in his mind every possibility and has been led to the un-shakeable conviction that believers in Christ are invincible: ". . . in all these things we are more than conquerors through him who loved us" (Rom. 8:37). From that follows the assurance that "nothing will be able to separate us from the love of God that is in Christ Jesus our Lord."

Surely attempts will be made but they shall never suc-ceed. The Lord is our keeper. He will never let us go.

If you have any doubts, consider what the Bible tells us.

Jesus was forsaken that we might never be forsaken. God purchased us to be his very own with the blood of his own dear Son. He dwells in our hearts through the Holy Spirit. All creatures, including our enemies, and all circumstances are under his control.

We are inseparably united with Christ. He is in us and we are in him. It is no more possible that believers should perish than that Christ himself should be dethroned.

The matter is settled. Nothing can separate us from the love of God. Glorious certainty!

Rejoice in your relationship to God. Rest in the assurance that you are his and his forever. Draw near to him with confidence and be strengthened in your conviction: No condemnation! No frustration! No separation! Amen and Hallelujah!